# 1000 Echos from the Thunder

## by

## Dr. Douglas Louie, Ph.D.

*Douglas Louie*
*2015*

ISBN      978-1-312-81220-8

# Forward

This autobiography has a down home feeling to it that is very reminiscent of Andy Griffin's Mayberry. The people in it are extraordinary in an ordinary way. Chester, the central character, is the most extraordinary and at the same time most humble. It is a joy to know him as portrayed in this volume, whether he's in Canada, Bar Harbor, Syracuse or Salisbury. Whether studying, teaching, saving souls, or building a recumbent bicycle from scratch; he carries with him the same genuine care and concern for the human condition.

I like his writing style. Simple, straight forward, without needless decorations or technical tricks for the sake of being clever. When I read the book, I feel relaxed, calm, as if I am in good hands on a pleasant journey, and all I have to do is sit back, relax, and leave the driving to the driver.

My favorite part is the chapter in which Dr. Louie expands on the importance of authenticity, transparency and vulnerability in relationships and marriage.

Richard Andersen
Author of We Called Him Bunny

# Prologue

## Profound Simplicity

# Table of Contents

# Chapter 1

## Great expectation

"Could you imagine the dinning table being leveled by a gold coin?" Grandma said to Chester one day.

"Wow."  Chester was wide eyed as a child on Christmas morning discovering his new toy under the Christmas tree.  He listened to the stories told about compatriots who returned to China after being away for many years.

"That would be the place I want to be when I grow up."  Chester was waiting for further description of this land called Gold Mountain. "  If it is so wonderful there, why would anyone want to leave and come back to this place?"

"They got lonely because they could not have their family with them.  Some of them got so desperate that they filed false immigration paper and claimed someone to be their bride or sons.  They were called 'paper son.'

"Tell me more about how they live and what Gold Mountain is like,"  Chester's curiosity was aroused and there was no stopping now.

"I don't know all the details but what they said sounded wonderful.  But Chester, someday you might have a chance to go there and see for yourself."  Grandma softly said to him, with a tiny bit of sadness
 anticipating the possible separation with her precious little bundle of joy.

"I will come back and visit you when I am able to put gold coins under your table."

"That would make my life complete."

Those were the thoughts in Chester's mind as he remembered Grandma talking about Gold Mountain. After three weeks crossing the Pacific Ocean, The Empress of Russia sighted lands. All anyone could see were trees with some small houses on the shore line. Surely that could not be the Gold Mountain Chester heard about. The apartment block he left had a lot more people than that. The tension was beginning to mount, wondering what Gold Mountain was really like. The ship was going as slowly as the turtle in Grandma's kitchen.

So far, the impression of Gold Mountain was anticlimactic after the stories he heard from Grandma and his cousins. The weather was dull and dreary. The sky was filled with clouds ready to pour out buckets of rain just like the summer hot day. "I should have stayed with Grandma, at least I can go to the stockyard and listen to the storyteller, especially when he jumped on the table and get excited about the cage being dropped around the rich merchant's bed when he was asleep."

Out of the blue, suddenly a loud thunderclap rang out in the sky. Raindrops started to fall gently until it developed into a full fledge thunderstorm. Everyone sought shelter. The thunder reverberated between the shores of the inlet. It was the first time in three weeks they had encountered any foul weather. The thunderclaps rang louder and louder until they became very uncomfortable. Everyone seem to be very upset, but not so with Chester. He remembered what his grandmother in Hong Kong told him when they were enjoying the quiet calm after a storm which came up regularly in the early evening. His grandmother explained to the young child that it was his forefathers greeting him and speaking to him. The young boy kept that thought seared in his mind and was able to enjoy the new experience of being on a ship sailing toward his destination. He made up a story in his mind that his forefathers was saying to him, "The future is before you, this is the start of a new life and adventure. There are many opportunities ahead of you, and if you're willing to work hard, any dreams you have can become true. The opportunities are there, this is Gold Mountain."

~

# Chapter 2

## The Mountain's there, but...

It is impossible to wipe clean nine years of one's life. It is only natural to compare new experiences with that which is familiar to you. When his father was bombarded by four persons, Chester's mother and three children, making references to the Hong Kong way of doing things, it irritated him so much that he forbade them ever to mention "Hong Kong" in his presence. This was extremely traumatic for this nine year old Chester. It meant forgetting the most significant persons in his life so far; to erase the happy times. Memories of the people he met and interacted with, the sound and smell of the apartment he occupied, the canary birds he helped to feed every morning. To wipe the slate clean as if it only happened in a dream, meant his sources of selfhood and security were lost. It had a long lasting effect on his personality. It was not until much later in life that Chester understood how dramatically this warped his life.

Their first house the family occupied in Vancouver was a small house on Keefer street in a narrow lot dwarfed by a four story wooden apartment house. The outside clapboard walls were unpainted showing neglect by the landlord. There was no more than thirty inches between the house and the open main walkway of the apartment. Frequently, mischievous children would bang on the window of the bedroom just to annoy his parents. Loud shuffling footsteps from drunks would be heard in the middle of the night as they tried to stumble and swaggered their way home.  Although he had never heard any complaints from his parents, Chester was very sure that more than once, they were awakened from their deep sleep in the wee hours of morning.

Speaking from "**Feng shui**" perspective, it was a poor living arrangement.  The house was damp and never saw direct sunlight.  It was always overshadowed by this monstrous four story tenement.  Chester had frequent colds and coughing.  As soon as possible, they moved to another house on Dunlevy Avenue where the situation improved somewhat.  Unfortunately it was next to a house belonging to a "lady of the night."  The only thing he remembered about this neighbor was her blood red painted fingernails as she  tapped on her window to attract men from the street during the day.  It was difficult for a drunken customer to differentiate between the row of identical houses, and his family frequently had a saliva dripping disheveled slobbering man banging on their door in the middle of the night wanting "service."

Although each of the three children had their own bed with mattresses, the one on Chester's bed must had been salvaged from the sidewalk, discarded because it was infested with bedbugs.  Since bedbugs were active only during the night, it was a long time before he could account for the source of bites on his body. Needless to say, the mattress was heaved to the sidewalk but it was quite awhile before they received an uncontaminated replacement that was donated by a member of the church.

The only excitement of the day for Chester as a child was to listen for the nine p.m. gun, fired at Prospect Point in

Stanley Park.  It was a tradition so that citizens of Vancouver could set their watches.

For amusement, he learned to entertain himself with materials around the house.  He remembered very vividly the time when he discovered how to whip the end of rope so it would not fray.  Instead of rope, he found the heaviest twine and used thread to do the winding.  That kept him entertained a long time and gave him much satisfaction when he was alone.

They as children had learned to sidestep their father's frugality.  His budget did not provide for recreation.  If they wanted to go to the theater, all they needed to say was that their teacher recommended it, and they could be assured of getting a ticket with no questions asked.

Adjustment in the Gold Mountain ran along two directions.  The first one was food. His father was either extremely frugal and/or conservative.  Varieties were not in his vocabulary at all.  Rice was the staple, the family ate rice three meals a day if possible and expected to be thankful.  If there were any complaints, the stock answer was, "be thankful for what you get.  There are people in China who are hungry and would kill for what we are having."  Breakfast was usually two pieces of toast with butter and grape jelly, washed down with a cup of green tea.  There would be cereal with milk to supplement the fare.  Lunch during school day would be two pieces of toast with butter and grape jelly.  Supper always included rice with some cooked leafy vegetable and some meat (usually fifteen cents worth of BBQ pork) bought from Chinatown.  Anything else would be considered a luxury beyond the budget.  The second direction of adjustment was adaptation to the new culture.  Generally during the 40's, immigrants and the general population in Chinatown believed strongly in maintaining their self identity and were very hostile to adaptation. For Chester, the process was complicated by the ultra conservatism of his parents.

Recreation was considered as non-essential to mental health. His father's idea of recreation was to go to the woodshed and chop wood for the kindling fire box. One was expected to apply himself to serious study and focus on the long term goal. To his father, the best way to learn English was to read the King James Version of the Bible. It was a good thing that Chester failed in that respect otherwise he would be speaking like a Quaker, using "I, thou and giv'st" instead of the everyday conversational vernacular. He was further admonished to spend more time in the library for there was no end to the reading material. Obviously he had no idea as to what could be found in the library. The classics were written in Elizabethan English or Chaucer style, while contemporary literature were written more in the vernacular.

It would appear that all of Chester's memories of his father was totally negative and included a heavy dose of anger and resentment toward him. Not so. Chester did appreciate his focus and perseverance toward bringing the family to the Gold Mountain in order to have better opportunities in life. There is a saying among the immigrants, "A dog on the street of Gold Mountain lives better than a rich man in China." Chester was sure that his father was referring to the things that everyone enjoyed in America, free education for every child, the safety nets provided by the government for the needy, (there were no beggars on the street except those who panhandled pedestrians) and the system of free enterprise, where one could create a fortune with a single original idea. Truly it was the Gold Mountain but one had to work hard for it. It was true that returning Chinese brought back gold coins to shim their dining room table, but history seldom mentioned the back breaking labor involved in building the transcontinental railroad by the immigrants, the danger of escaping methane gas explosions causing lost of life, and the ridicule and racism that existed in this hostile land. Life for the early immigrants was not all glitz and glamor, one must be willing to dig for the gold.

His father's strong emphasis on education was laudable. He saw that was the only way to get out of the doldrums of being an immigrant. He must have done a good job on Chester for he spent much time in classrooms and won the highest academic honor available.. He never regretted pursuing that goal for it added much to his self esteem and self satisfaction.

~

# Chapter 3

## Transition

In Chester's family, the highest priority of life was to get an education. All the planning and decisions on the macro and micro level were made on the question "Does it help to achieve that objective?" That was the sole reason for the hardship of immigrating from the east to the west. The primary stage of achieving this objective was the mastery of the English language, both written and oral.

Their family lived a very insularly existence. His father believed in keeping a very low profile, if you stayed low and in the corner, you would not be noticed and you would not be harassed. Consequently, the children were not allowed to play on the street or mix with other children in the neighborhood. Little did he know that that was the only way to learn English. To him, the Bible was good enough for the church for two thousand years, so it must be good for his children. It was impossible for someone without driving experience to teach another how to drive. Such was the case for him, he never spoke English himself, nor tried to learn the language. Everything he knew about English was by osmosis from his cousins and nephews who operated the grocery wholesale business in Vancouver. Though they were Canadian born, they were too busy managing the business to spend any time to mentor their older uncle who was ultra conservative in attitudes toward adaptation to another culture. Chester's family was too close to Chinatown and too comfortable in this self contained community to feel any need to venture beyond Pender and Keefer street neighborhood..

The first thing Chester must learn about English was that it was a mongrel language. It borrowed from other sources. Common words like "forté", "deja-vu", "carte blanche'" were borrowed from the French; "andantè" from Italian,"autobahn" from German, and "schlep" from Yiddish, "antibody" from Greek and others from Latin. English had component parts like prefix and suffix, vowels (aeiou) and consonants (d,f,k) , tenses in verbs (sing,sang, sung), numbers in nouns (focus,foci),and idioms (hurry up, when you are downstairs already). All that was foreign in the Chinese language.

Pronunciation was a great hurdle for Chester. Each Chinese character had five intonations, each one was used according to context. Each English polysyllabic word owned an accent for proper pronunciation (for example, "resuscitation."). Neither would you always pronounce words as they were spelled (coup-de grace), and at other times they silenced an alphabet (Graham) and even truncate words as in "Westminister" and "basically."

Learning the oral part of the language was only half of the picture. The other half was the mastery of idioms. That was learned only by being in the company of indigenous people who were native to the country. Phrases did not always make sense, but the use of similes and metaphors added color and a greater depth of appreciation of the situation. "Busy as a bee" was a good example. No number of words or combination of words could convey the aura of persistence, determination, and focus of the group as that phrase would. You could almost hear the droning and the buzzing around the bee hives without another word.

Also, no words were adequate to suggest more the texture of a certain surface than to say : "smooth as the baby's bottom." Finally, to present the impossible case, the seriousness and certainty of a point was made by using the idiom "till hell freezes over." There was no doubt that the final argument had been made when someone said, "end of discussion."

The only way to learn the vernacular was to learn it while playing and speaking with other kids. But Chester's learning was limited to contact only at school. Chester's most vivid memories of such instructions took place in the waiting room to the men's restroom in the Presbyterian church among his cousins. He was a bi-linguist all through elementary and high school and throughout his undergraduate study. This certainly delayed his learning process of the new language.

There were various levels of mastery of a new language. The first level was the verbal, to be understood by others. But the Chinese language was so dissimilar to English, that immigrants from China worked out a pseudo combination of both, commonly called "chinglish." It was an adaptation of speaking English according to the Chinese intonation of words and sentence construction without paying attention to accent and sounding "th" and other suffixes like "d and f." Chinglish often left out verbs; it did not have to deal with the peculiarity of the third person verbs. They knew nothing of conjugation of irregular verbs and the idea of tenses was absent from the language. Sometimes it was called "pigeon English". The second level of mastering the language was to concentrate on the written part of English. It required concentration to the details and to learn by reading written materials, something which most immigrants did not have a chance to do. But the highest level of mastery of the English language was to be able to exploit its beauty and the richness and considered communication as an art form. This was achieved by using metaphors and similes to add color and intensity to your writing. This was a luxury seldom mastered by immigrants. By learning the verbal part only, it was sufficient to assure them of employment in restaurants and domestic services like gardening.

As long as Chester was living at home, he spoke Chinese to accommodate his parents as familial loyalty to them. His father applied the same rule of pronunciation to English as in Chinese. Chester remembered the only time his father attempted to teach him English was when he demonstrated how to pronounce "determine." He used the same "sing-song" manner as in "sing-sang-sung" without awareness of placing the accent on the second syllable. When Chester copied his style, he became the laughing stock in school for a whole week.

Pronunciation was a huge obstacle for Chester to overcome. Years later, this was driven home when during the word recognition software prior to the modern version **"dragon"** came on the market. The machine could not acknowledge some of the words Chester input into the database. After too many rejections, he gave up the idea of shortcutting the process from speaking to typing manually on the keyboard. He threw out a ninety nine dollars investment.

Chester consulted experts on how to minimize the Chinatown influence on his speech. "Did Winston Churchill have an accent? Everyone has one. Learn to live with it and just be yourself. There are other attractive things about you to celebrate that can detract from any focus on your diction." This helped him immensely and he began to enjoy the unique singularity of who he was. It was empowering to be recognized over the phone as soon as he spoke his name, because there was only one who spoke like "Chester."

~

# Chapter 4

## A silver dollar in his pocket

The sun sneaked out of hiding at the horizon at 5 am in the morning, when Chester stepped out into the damp summer air. He headed for the rendezvous with an open deck delivery truck which would bring him to spend a day in the blistering sun to pick strawberries for a farmer. Fifteen sleepy heads mounted to the deck of the truck, each one wrapped in raggedy overalls and a wide brim hat, trying to find a place on the hard bench on each side of the vehicle. There was no conversation among the women, each one deep in her own thoughts. There was no time to waste, for the route was forty five minute ride through the city streets. The street was deserted during that early hour of the day. It was like a coaster ride at Disneyland along the bumpy road except for an occasional jarring stop at the traffic lights. They arrived at the farm promptly at ten minutes before six. Without any instruction, each one moved like a robot, picking up a ten quart basket and heading toward rows of strawberry plants. In silence they picked the ripe berries and put them gingerly in the basket. There was only one rule, "leave the green ones alone for another day." For today, they looked for the big ripe ones without any blemishes. Meanwhile the sun climbed higher and higher in the cloudless sky and within half an hour, they began to feel the warmth on their back and their hands. The wise and experience ones took care to cover their exposed skin for the sun can leave its footprint like bigfoot in the movies. It would cause a sunburn when you were in the sun for ten hours. It was hard to find a comfortable position to work. After a few minutes of kneeling, your knees began to feel the rough weeds beneath you. You then changed to a crouching position until you felt the stretch on your legs and thighs. Even though it was a no brainer job, it was hard work. After the first basket was filled, you looked forward to walking upright if only for a short distance to bring the basket to the truck and pick up an empty one to repeat the harvest. It was a job suitable for children because there was a shorter distance between their shoulders and the ground. After a while, the welcome sound of a bell was heard to summon the workers to come for their 10 o'clock morning break. Soft bread never tasted so good with butter and jam on top. The tea was warm, just the right temperature to wash down the food. Casual conversation appeared sparingly among the women.

"Was your husband still asleep when you left this morning?"

"He worked the night shift cooking in a restaurant and did not get back to the house until 4 in the morning. We just managed to say 'hello and goodbye' to each other."

"What a way to live. It is a hard life to earn a living these days."

"And they say, 'this is the Gold Mountain.' I just hope that we can stay healthy without any sickness in our family."

"Morning break is now over and we better get back to work before our boss starts to complain about the price he is getting from the store."

So everyone took the last sip of tea and headed back to the field.

By noon time, everyone was sweating profusely under the 90 degree heat.  Lunchtime could not have come too soon.  To get some relief from the sun under a clear sky, each one sought out a shady spot to eat their lunch.  The farm was the delta, created by the soil that was washed down by the Fraser River.  There were no trees, except those planted by farmers to break up the landscape.  Chester's back was beginning to get uncomfortable.  For the first five minutes, he just laid on his back on the bare ground.  Gradually his muscles would relax and he could sit upright to eat his sandwich of bologna and cheese.  His mouth was as dry as the week old stale bread.  There was not enough saliva to chew the sandwich until he drank a mouthful of ginger ale.  Things gradually changed until he felt the hunger pain inside him. He began to eat the two sandwiches with gusto.  It was good to have a few minutes of rest on his back again until the women got up together like a flight of birds on their annual southward migration.  They covered themselves again from the glistening sun and worked quietly until 3 o'clock in the afternoon when bread and butter and jam were served.  Many chose to find a shade to rest rather than eat because it was too close to their supper time at 6:30 at home.  Two more hours of sweltering heat in the sun and the long awaited quitting time came at 5:30.  Each one was given a silver dollar as wages for the day's work.  They were herded into the truck which delivered them back to the rendezvous point in the city.

As Chester was jostling along, he was aware that the cuticles of his fingers were broken and began to bleed a little.  Nevertheless, he reminded himself that this was another way to mine for gold in the gold mountain, only he found a silver coin instead.

So they did the same thing all over again the next day.

Chester was happy to find work at the farm. It was hard for an eleven year old boy to find employment in the city because they were considered under age. After the strawberry crop was done, they could stay to pick carrots, beans, potatoes and turnips. This would keep them busy until school days started up again.

During school time and weekends,they could find work washing dishes in the restaurants, busing in the dining room, clerking in a Mom and Pop fresh produce stores and even waiting on tables. If you were willing to work , there were jobs around, although some were quite menial like peeling carrots and peeling potatoes to make french fries.

Work was traditional in the family, they received no allowance as other children might. There were no luxuries like spending money for ice cream or for buying candies. If they wanted any extra money, they worked for it. Any wages the children received they kept in their own account. They were encouraged to work hard and to fulfill the cultural admonition, "All work is honorable." The mantra in the family was "work hard, save up your money so you can go to 'big school'." Beside it was the legitimate way of getting out of the house. Every spare moment, weekends and holiday, Chester worked. All through elementary school, high school, undergraduate study, if Chester was not attending school, he would be found working. His first break was after ordination after study at St. Andrew's.

They were poor without knowing they were poor. Chester's wardrobe was extremely spartan. He did not have a bureau to put his personal clothing until he lived in a dorm at St. Andrew's. He arrived at Vancouver with one suitcase in his hand and he lived out of that suitcase all through elementary, high school and his undergraduate days. He came to Vancouver wearing a tropic outfit of a white shirt, a pair of white shorts, white socks and tennis shoes. The first shopping was done at Woodward Department Stores. His father bought him a long sleeve shirt, a pair of long trousers, and a pair of shoes. This was reserved as his Sunday best. His everyday school clothes were all hand-me-downs. Chester remembered having a lightweight sweater for the cooler weather. Later on, his cousin gave him a sport jacket with a wide band sewn around the back at the waistline. It was so "dated" in the Great Gatsby era that he refused to wear it at all. That was replaced by a donated black sport jacket which he wore from grade 4 to college graduation. He was given discarded socks from his father, by which he inherited athlete's foot and it stayed with him all through his life. He always wore a scarf because of the damp winter, indoor and outdoor and a black tie with his shirt. His only pair of trousers was worn until the seat was threadbare and it was patched with a white sugar sack. He accepted the idea of wearing hand-me-downs as normal until he was called to go to the chalkboard in Grade 6 when thirty pairs of eye were trying to decipher the manufacturer's name shown through the patchwork of his seat. That was the most humiliating moment of his life. He felt like he would rather be banished to the island of Elba than having to appear before the classmates again. Chester forgot how that awkward situation was resolved, but somehow he managed to survive it. So that was the lowest point of Gold Mountain experiences, the rest has to be better, there was no other direction to go but up.

Black or cream

"Black or cream" was the greeting instead of "Good morning" to the customers who came to this Chinatown café shop where Chester was working. Imagine saying that forty thousand times in the eight hours behind a thirty foot counter, serving coffee to customers all day.

Each Saturday and Sunday morning during the school year, he would get up at 4 in the morning and he then walked a short distance to Hong Kong Cafe. Chester liked his early shift because it left most of the afternoon for himself. One became a perpetual motion machine the moment he stepped into the building. Being young and full of energy. At that age, it was no big deal for a growing boy. He just made up his mind to keep moving for the next eight hours to keep his boss happy. Although it was damp or foggy outside, it was always warm and well lit inside the cafe shop. The floor was soft and spongy to walk on, which added a bouncy feeling to his steps as if he was walking on air. From behind the counter, he could see one long stretch of wooden counter top with a shiny patina from years of constant cleaning and polishing each time a customer left his seat. There must have been thirty stools on the other side of the counter; one never bothered to count. All one cared about was to make sure the customer's cup was filled to the brim. The menu was very simple, they served only coffee, and the cakes and sandwiches were displayed behind glass door. The choice of beverage was very simple, with or without cream. It was just like the early models of Ford cars, you can have any color you want as long as it is black. There were many cafe shops to choose from in Chinatown. It seemed that each shop featured their own signature blend of coffee. The highlight of the day was when the hot cross buns came out of the oven; you could smell them a mile away. That was the time when people would come in like the Mongolian invaders ravishing the land. The buns disappeared as soon as they were brought from the kitchen to the dining area. Customers devoured them like hungry wolves even when they were too hot to handle by the waiters.

A typical customer was a male worker, who kept a bachelor pad without any kitchen. He was in Canada by himself without his wife. Though he might be already married in China. Many of them lived in common law relationships with a woman out of sheer loneliness.


## Early working days

Chester's early working experience had always been connected with the food industry, particularly in the kitchen. He started washing dishes in a restaurant, then he had a job cleaning potatoes and preparing French fries while he was in high school. By that time, when he was comfortable around the kitchen, he was making salads and sandwiches. He was then befriended by his uncle at Mount Shasta Cafe and mentored by a chef in his eighties. You might say that everything Chester knew about cooking, he learned mostly from him. Chester prepared the breakfast menu under his watchful eyes while the master prepared for the lunch menu. He was most patient and wise. Chester did not make too many mistakes. After the breakfast crowd disappeared, the luncheon patrons came in. They were mostly working class, law enforcement officers and laborers. After he gained experience under the master's tutorage and gradually became proficient as a short order cook, he even felt like they were a team working well together.

During the second Christmas holiday, while making a salad, Chester had an out of body experience. Though it was of very short duration, nevertheless, he felt completely detached from his physical body, looking down from the ceiling, and asked himself why was he picking up this handful of peas and not carrots? Was he adding enough salad dressing to the dish? As suddenly as he entered into this detached state, he was united once more with his body. It was a frightening but novel and strange experience. The thought did occur to Chester that he might be losing his mind. Soon this strange possibility disappeared but the memory remained in his mind as vivid today as when it happened sixty plus years ago.

Chester enjoyed his day off, at which time he frequented Stanley Park and it was there that he was introduced to bagpipe music. The sound was melancholic but it had a strong uplifting beat which conveyed energy and power. He felt quite at home, and appreciated the genius of just by adding one note, the music changed from the C natural key to a minor key. As he approached closer to the actual players, he was enthralled by the flourishes of the mallet of the tenor drummers in unison and precision. It just lifted his spirit, and Chester was moved to the far and misty heather hills of Scotland. He promised himself that somehow he was going to play that instrument on some hilltops in America. This dream never left him. It was many years later that he owned a set of bagpipes. He was in Ridgeway Ontario Canada, when the dream was fulfilled.

On his day off, he generally meandered around town aimlessly. He would have liked to take more trips to the many attractions in Vancouver, but there was no companion. He heard so much about Harrison Hot Spring and decided to take the bus trip. After an hours ride, it stopped at the spring. It was absolutely barren, not even a store in sight. It was like being dropped off in the middle of the Sahara desert in Africa. There was no office depot. He was extremely disappointed with the trip. All he could do was to sit on the lonely park bench and wait for the bus to take him back to the city. That was the first and only excursion trip he took by himself.

While working in the kitchen, he could have any food he wanted for his meal; chicken, seafood, meat, roast. But looking at food all day, they held no mystery for him. His favorite dish was a thin slice of halibut, sufficiently cooked and with lemon and ketchup. It is better than any steak or chicken.

The pastry chef showed him how to make pies and particularly Boston Cream pie. He always helped him to whip up the cream topping and was always the one to clean up the copper bowl with his fingers.

Working around the kitchen was an excellent experience for Chester  According to the Chinese culture, the attributes of a scholar gentleman is he must be able to wield the wok and skillet as well as the brush in calligraphy and painting.

~

# Chapter 5

## A chink in her armor

Chester was enrolled at Strathcona Elementary School in September and was placed in the third grade with Miss Swanson as his teacher. He was learning English as a new language as well as other subjects like Social Studies. Certain particular items of the curriculum stood out, such as the names of the four seasons, spelling, English grammar and science. Arithmetic came easy to him and he was quite advanced to the rest of the class. He committed almost everything to memory, so it turned out that he was third student from the top, in a class of thirty.

In the fourth grade, there was one class a week where each student could choose a special interest group. There were groups like cooking, commercial typing, sewing; but he chose journalism. The school put out a monthly newspaper for the fourth grade. Everyone in this group had to write a little paragraph to candidate for the position of editor of the paper. On his paper, there were many corrections with words crossed out and phrases were put at a different place by using arrows. Though corrected, it left a very untidy paper, telling the teacher that he wasn't very sure of himself. Needless to say, he was not chosen to be the editor.

Chester skipped grade five and went to grade six, missing the first three weeks of work. Thinking back, for some strange reason, he just felt that time was running out, and that he had to finish grade school as soon as possible. There must have been great pressure at home, though unspoken, that since he was the youngest of the children, he was the caboose of the train, and that he was dragging his feet. He could not be any more definite than that. Anyway, the pressure was bad enough that he voluntarily spoke to his teacher and told her what he wanted. She consulted with the principal, and he was moved to Grade six.

Reflecting back on the incidence, Chester had other insights to explain what he did. He was never able to please his father. He never received any encouragement to know that he was approved of for any of his efforts. He remembered when he brought back a report card with all A's and only one B, his father asked Chester why there was a B. The explanation was that in gym, he was unable to do a headstand. Thus he received a B. His father could not accept that reason and saw no reason why he cannot do a headstand. So Chester was constantly seeking ways to please him and to get his endorsement. In his innocence, he finally came up with the idea that if he could only skip a grade in school, surely that was something he could appreciate since he valued education so much. Strangely enough, not a word was mentioned. This insensitivity gradually grew to resentment and detachment.

Grade six was a fun year for Chester. The teacher's name is Miss C. He remembered her very well. She was the prettiest of all the teachers he had. However she did have her moments of frustration with the class. One time she lost her cool, and made reference to the bookcase which her father made especially for her. Chester forgot the connection between the situation in class and the bookcase, but the mention of her father stuck in his mind. Even at that young age, he thought it was a disconnect between the situation and her father. Another incidence remained in his mind.  They were discussing the progress made from one generation to another.  The question was posed, "Do you think that we are smarter than our forefathers?"  Chester raised his hand and answered, "yes, that is how new things were discovered and things were improved."  He was shot down in no uncertain terms in front of his whole class.  He was told that that was extremely disrespectful to speak of them in that way.  We should be more aware of the good they did for us, etc, etc. From then on, Chester totally disengaged himself from her and never raised his hands to volunteer any answer in her class.  However he found other outlets in school.

He found he had a special affinity for Science.  The teacher was Miss Sutherland.  She had one peculiar way of teaching.  Later after many years of graduate school and writing term papers, Chester understood why accuracy in terms of spelling and punctuation were so important.  She insisted that her students learn this lesson in her class.

She had a unique way of teaching accuracy and proper reporting.  She would ask each student to write the report and present it to her to check for proper spelling, grammatical construction and correct sentence construction.  If she found a mistake, she would make a check mark at the right hand margin and send the student back to his seat, to find the mistake himself, and stand at the line to wait for his turn at her desk.  There was no hint as to the nature of the mistake to be corrected.  Smart ones like Chester reacted to this inefficient way of teaching, sought ways to shortcut this process by erasing her pencil mark and put his own mark near the end of the report hoping that the teacher would accept the location of the check mark as indication that all material written up to that point was correct.  Her eagle eyes went back to the last erased check mark and marked the mistake. All this was done without her saying a word. Chester soon learned that their teacher wasn't born yesterday, that she knew all the tricks of youngsters and probably she had done them herself when she was younger. In spite of the games they played, she became his favorite teacher during his elementary school experience.

It was at the time, he took an interest in performing experiments on his own. He learned how to produce magnetism by running an electric current through a piece of wire wrapped around a metal object. Secretly, he secured a piece of discarded wire from a lamp cord, wrapped it around a nail driven into a piece of wood, stripped the ends of the wire and plugged them into the electric socket. He turned the switch on and nothing happened. Only a flash of blue light came from the wall and he blew the fuse in the electric panel for the house. Everyone in the house came rushing in to see if anyone was hurt, fearing the worst, that someone might have been electrocuted. Everyone felt relieved to see no one was hurt. Of course Chester dismantled his experiment as fast as he could, but not completely. He left enough clues for his brother to figure out what he was attempting to do. The mystery was solved, but the strangest thing happened, he was not punished, not even scolded. Nothing more was said and it was never mentioned again.

Grade seven was uneventful but grade eight was the highlight of Strathcona. The outstanding event was to be able to take up manual art, a chance to work with tools. They learned the fundamentals of reading drawings, plan and elevation, and a chance to work with hand tools like saws and planes. As a special project, Chester made a footstool.  Without any help or instruction, intuitively he knew how to make mortise and tenon joints at the four corners of the stool.  When he brought it home to show his father, he did not get one word of encouragement or acknowledgment.  Though it was a great disappointment, nevertheless, it started a life long interest in woodworking and tools for him.

Toward the second half of eighth grade, families and children of Japanese ancestry were evacuated from the west coast and relocated to the interior of British Columbia to work on beet farms.  Children who were born in Canada,who knew no other country, were not exempted.  It was a time of mass hysteria, and proved to be a shameful chapter of Canadian and American history.  Though the Japanese people in Canada were officially offered a public apology many years after the end of the WWII, the lump sum settlement given to all internees could never erase the loss of livelihood and property suffered by the victims.  Chester could feel the confusion and anger suffered by the children in his school.  They were all gentle people and kept their feelings to themselves.

~

# Chapter 6

## New Adventure

Chester jumped out of bed this morning. He was very excited because today was the day he worked toward for five years. At last his dream came true. He was going to take his first streetcar ride all by himself. He no longer lived under the shadow of his older siblings. He no longer had to "live up to the family's standards." He was free to be himself. Beginning that day he felt quite grown up.

After the usual breakfast of tea and toast, he even added an egg on his plate because he did not know what to expect, he did not know when or where he would have lunch. He made sure that the knot of his necktie was in the best possible shape, straightened out his white shirt, brushed his teeth with extra effort, and headed out the door.

Today, he was going to start high school, to King Edward High at that. He felt so proud of himself that he was not going to Britannia High, where his siblings were going. He looked forward to striking out on his own, to a place where he was given a chance to be known for who he was and not "Oh, you are Kwong's younger brother. I hope you are as good a student as he is."

The streetcar he was waiting for finally came to his corner and he climbed on board. Gave his dollar bill to the conductor to buy the student tickets.

"Going to school, young man?" the streetcar conductor started the small talk.

"Yes, to King Edward High School."

"You know where it is, I am sure."

"I would like for you to call out the street for me, Sir. I won't want to miss the corner."

"Listen for Oak street. That will be your stop."

"Thank you Sir."

Chester took his seat right next to the door and made sure that he could hear him call out the street.

It was "Maple" then "Oak Street." That was his signal.

He nearly jumped out of his skin when he got off the street car. He was nearing his new school.

He had to walk three blocks uphill to get to the school. The building was surrounded with a spacious football field, green with grass, meticulously trimmed like a pencil line etched on a drafting board. The building was made of stone, two stories high, rather old looking. As soon as he stepped in, everything appeared nice and bright. There was a clean smell of paint and the light colored hardwood floor was newly varnished. Each of the doors had a fresh coat of paint in different colors. At the entrance of the main door was a sign "All new students with names A to M. Room 104, Names from N to Z, Room 106."

"That was easy enough" he said to himself. "I am going to enjoy this."

He found Room 104 and walked in to join twenty students already chatting among themselves. There were blonds and redheads among them and immediately he noticed that he was the only Asian in the room. After he took a seat, the boy with freckled face next to him smiled. Chester smiled back.

"Are we at the right place? My name starts with L, what is yours?"

"Mine starts with M, McLean. What is yours?"

"Mine starts with L, Louie.  Nice to meet you."

At that very moment, a man with a new suit entered and introduced himself.

"I am Mr. Blake the Vice principal of this school.  I want to welcome you to our school.  I hope you will enjoy your next four years with us.  Today is going to be very short, just some paper work to get you registered with us and to give you the class schedule for tomorrow. Everything is self explanatory.  Everyone has a pencil? Please fill in the registration form and hand it to me when you finish and pick up your class schedule."  He proceeded to pass out the paper and took his seat behind the teacher's desk in front.

The form asked the usual questions like home address and telephone number, father's name and so on. When Chester finished his, he approached Mr. Blake and gave him his paper.  He seemed to have picked him out in advance, because he called him by name.

"Welcome Louie, Strathcona School told us you would be coming and asked us to take good care of you. They said that you are one of their shining stars."

As he briefly glanced at the paper from top to bottom, he said, "Good job!..Welcome again. If you have any problems, come to see me.  My door is always open."

"Thank you, Sir."

"Here is your class schedule.  See you tomorrow."

After Chester left the room, he wandered down the hall and tried to locate the rooms for the classes tomorrow. The rooms were all on the first floor and they were right next to each other.

"Piece of cake," he said to himself.

As he left the building, he found himself having to weave between bunches of students in small groups excitedly exchanging experiences of the summer.

One girl took a trip to Las Vegas with her family. "and you know what, I won a jackpot of thirty dollars at the slot machine. That was fun. I could hardly tear myself from the machine after that."

Another was showing off her sun tanned arms to her friends "We took a cruise to the Bahamas......."

"And I took a trip to the farm everyday and picked turnips," Chester thought to himself.

He proceeded to find his way back to the same street car stop. Already there was a small group waiting, chattering about their summer activities. The car came without any delay and they all were herded into the vehicle like sheep; just follow the leader.

After a long ride, he arrived back home. Once again, he smelled the stench from the false creek at the end of Georgia Street and the smoke of the railroad engine from Great Northern Railroad.

When he got home, no one met him at the door, no one asked him about his adventure and everyone carried on with the usual routine as if nothing special had happened. But he knew it was a red letter day for him. It was the day he started to cut the apron strings and was beginning to do things on his own. That was a good feeling of self confidence and power. Chester slept good that night.

The years spent at King Edward High were an eye opener in many respects. For the first time he had a chance to see how the "other side of the tracks" looked . The school was located in the upper middle class area of Vancouver. Instead of smelling the ammonia gas leaking from the sausage factory on the way home for lunch and the scums of the dry dock at the end of Georgia Street, nice houses on neatly trimmed lawns and exquisite flower beds surrounded the school. In the spring, windows were opened to catch the gentle breeze and he could hear piano music; someone playing Bach. As he walked around the neighborhood after he ate his lunch of bread and peanut butter, he was impressed with the contrast between the haves and the have nots. He had a dream then that someday he would live at that level of elegance. Meanwhile as he struggled through two years of German, he had not yet obtained command of the English language as he should have.

He had a teacher named Mr. Coolwater for his Chemistry class. His head was bald as the baby's bottom. He exchanged his weekend escapade with one of his students.

"Did you catch any good ones at the cottage last weekend?"

"You should have been there when this big one got away. I swear it must have been a four pound wide mouth bass. I struggle with him for a good thirty minutes. When I got him close enough to the boat and was ready to net him, he jerked away from my line. You should have seen him. Too bad, and I didn't even have a picture to show you."

"That is the way it is, you win some and you lose some."

"Isn't that the truth."

This went on for many weeks. His eager students in his class went ahead and read the textbook themselves and then studied on their own. Sometimes, they deliberately interrupted his conversation with a question hoping that would give him a hint that he should be teaching their class Chemistry. It was useless. It wasn't until near the end of the semester that he got down to the serious business of teaching how to balance the valences in a chemical equation.

By that time, his teaching served as a review for Chester for he had already learned on his own.

Chester took German as his choice of foreign language for high school graduation. There were three boys in the class. The other boys were David and Donald. All three boys became good friends, exchanging homework, helping each other when one was in difficulty. One day they were working on a project and Chester was invited to have lunch at David's home.

"Would you like to come to my house, have lunch with us and we can finish the project afterwards?"

"That sounds like a good idea."

"My house is not far from the school. Lets go, I am hungry, are you?"

David lived a short distance from the school and there was no hurry to return back to school. It was quite an experience for Chester. It was the first time that he found himself in an English speaking home and he observed the interaction between different generations.

"Did you have a good day in school, David?" his mother asked.

"We three boys were given a project and we did not have enough time to complete it. So I asked my friend Chester to come and have lunch with us, so we can finish the project together."

"Well Hello, Chester, glad you can join us for lunch. Let me set another place at the table for you boys. You must be famished by now. And Donald, always nice to see you. Glad to have you with us today."

David's mother went ahead and set the third place mat on the table and put another piece of meat in the frying pan without a word. It seem like this kind of situation happened all the time. Chester immediately felt the ease with which he was made to feel at home. Intuitively, he knew the atmosphere in this home was very relaxed, children were valued and accepted, and they were allowed to grow at their own pace. There was an abundance of gentleness, and caring was aplenty in this house. And secretly he wished that his home life enjoyed the same serenity and security.

It was at this time that he began to notice girls around him. For the first time, he was in close proximity with girls with blond hair. Many wore their hair pony tail style, tied high on top of their head. Chester screamed silently when he saw their hair undulate from side to side as they walked down the hall. Up to this time, all women he knew with long hair always appeared with a braided pigtail style. A few would wind their pigtail into a ball and pin it at the back of their head. It was quite a new experience for a fourteen year old freshman to be in the same class in Chemistry with these mature young ladies. Needless to say, they provided much distraction but he always kept his distance and beheld them as goddesses until the examination score showed they were just students like him. In fact, he learned that he had a steeper learning curve than they.

Like all teens, he liked to look mature and sophisticated. Thinking that macho men always were seen with a cigarette in their mouth, he started to smoke. It was his friend Bobby who said calmly to him without any emotion, "You don't need that to look grown up." Chester knew what he meant. He threw his third unfinished cigarette in the gutter and never smoked again. Thanks to his friend Bobby (wherever you are) for helping him to quit this filthy habit.

During this time, all the boys in school were organized into a cadet corp. One period a week was reserved for cadet training. Chester elected to learn Morse Code. He soon showed himself to be very fast at reading the signal since he took it as his hobby and practicing with his brother. He soon lost interest in what they were doing until he was asked to do the sending. He took a book and was reading the paragraph backward and sending the letters backward. Nobody figured out the source of his message, and Chester kept it a secret until today.

~

# Chapter 7

## Moose Jaw Collegiate

Chester finished his high school study in Moose Jaw, Saskatchewan, when his father moved from Vancouver B C to work with the United Church of Canada in Saskatchewan Conference. He spent two years there and completed Grade 12, which was the equivalent of Senior Matriculation in the British Columbia province standard. The Moose Jaw Collegiate was a college track preparatory school, with an emphasis on standard classical curriculum. It lacked a gymnasium and an auditorium for student activities. The winter weather was a big issue and the heating bill for the building must have been horrendous. For native dwellers, 40 degree below zero weather was considered invigorating and ice hockey predominated the sport scene among young and old alike. Bonspiel and curling were the favorite pastime during winter when contestants would get up 3 o'clock in the morning to play a game.

During his days in King Edward High School days, he was taking correspondence courses with the hope of shortening the four years high school into three. These additional studies exempted him from some of the classes in Saskatchewan curriculum. Thus he had many study hall periods in the afternoon. Some afternoon it was all study hall, so instead of staying in the basement of the school, he found himself at the nearby skating rink and spent his afternoon skating instead. It was during this period he joined the Sea Cadet Corps and attended their parade every Thursday night. They had two ship companies plus a bugle band. The activities in the regular group did not prove to be too serious, very little seamanship was actually taught to the boys. They were focused on learning morse code which Chester mastered in King Edward High in Vancouver. Joining the bugle band was the only alternative. He was given a bugle to learn to play the scale. He did not receive much instruction on how to play the instrument, except that he was supposed to practice and practice some more. He managed to play a few notes, but not with any consistency. However it was better than to waste his time with the kids playing games. The cadet corps was headed by a Lieutenant in an officers' uniform and he had a Chief Petty Officer assisting him. This left a vacancy to work in the quartermaster store in charge of the uniforms and equipment. They invited Chester to fill the spot. Unfortunately the Petty Officer rank does not go with the responsibility, so he declined. During this time, V-J Day was celebrated and the Sea Cadet was invited to march in the parade in Moose Jaw. Fireworks lighted up the sky and much music was heard that evening.

The first summer he spent in Moose Jaw, he worked in the kitchen of one of the larger restaurants in the city as a helper. He was assigned to make French fries for fish and chips. He had a crush on one the young ladies working there as a soda bar clerk. She was pretty, and he found out later that her father was the school superintendent in a university city. As the summer drew to a close, he asked her if he could write to her. His first letter was a casual letter, relating to the normal routine of starting school and making new friends. It was nothing serious at all. She returned his letter with all the corrections on his grammatical errors with red ink with no additional note of her own.  He didn't know what to make of it.  It puzzled him to find an explanation, whether she was out to prove her superiority or she wished to supplement the English instructions he was getting.  He could not tell whether she intended to continue the correspondence or not.  It was a crushing blow to his ego, especially with a fragile self esteem typical of a teenager.  He did not make any further contact with her.

At Grade twelve, every student received an I.Q. test to fulfill requirement of a guidance counseling session.  When the principal called  Chester to his office for a review of his test score and his future career goal, Mr A. left his seat behind his desk and came around to Chester's side, draped his arm around his shoulder and softly said to him,

"And Chester, what do you hope to be when you grow up?"

"I was thinking about studying Medicine," he replied.

" I would not be so ambitious if I were you.  I would be so happy if you can graduate from my school.  You did not do that well in your I.Q. test, you only scored 86 points."

As a footnote, Chester called it "sweet revenge" when Mr. A was present at his ordination after finishing his study in Theology.  Though it was not to be, he wished very much that he would be able to witness the Convocation ceremony when he receive his Ph.D. Degree with 46,000 sitting in the Carrier Dome in Syracuse NY applauding.

~

# Chapter 8

## U B C

His years spent in undergraduate study at the University of British Columbia was a major part of Chester's life as he slowly matured and learned the ways of the real world. It was then that he began to cut the apron string, grew spiritually, had a chance to developed his own personality, and be more aware of his strength and vulnerability, and generally "try to spread his wings a bit." He had many good mentors who were kind and helpful and wished he had many more.

Ever since grade nine, he had always worked on weekends and holidays. He started out serving coffee in Hong Kong Cafe, or washing dishes in restaurants, and eventually became a short order cook in Mount Shasta Cafe. He learned about frugality from his parents and every cent he earned, he saved it and put it in the bank. By the time he was ready to register for his first year at the university, he proudly produced a hundred dollar bill for two semesters and still got one dollar back in change. The value of the dollar was quite different in the 40's.

Even before he worked as the server in the coffee shop, he went with his uncle in his model-T truck peddling produce to stay at home moms. He learned to take orders and make change as he delivered fruits and vegetable to the women. A particular elderly woman took a special liking to him and asked how he was getting along in school.

"What is your best subject?" Mrs. Harding inquired.
"I am quite good in Math and Science."

"Which one you find the hardest?"

"I would say English literature." This was while he was in Grade seven.

The next time he went to her house, after the business of selling was finished, Mrs. Harding said, "I have something for you." She handed him an anthology of Shakespeare's work.

He thanked her politely and accepted her gift. Later on at home, he started to read the book and it all sounded so strange, it bore no resemblance to the text books he used in school. It was difficult to understand Mrs. Harding's gift, except that she meant well and wanted to encourage him as much as she could. She even invited him to come to skiing with the family, but he knew that he did not fit into that circle and would feel out of place like a road-kill on the highway.

The university was located in a very spacious and scenic tract of land of Point Grey. According to a visiting professor from Oxford, who had traveled all over the world, he considered U B C to rank among the most scenic campuses in the world. It was bordered on the three sides with the water of the Puget Sound and one could see the mountains of North Vancouver without moving your feet at all. There was a golf course on the ground providing the best recreation available.

Engineering students were sent out to perfect their surveying skill as they mapped out the ground of the institution. Many of them were reported to have ended up into Prince Rupert, 400 miles north. Many took their lunch and walking a short distance and sat on the beach just on the other Marine Drive to enjoy the water. It was near the close of the WW II, when there was a flood of returned veterans.

The student body swelled suddenly and expansion took place at a frentic rate. They were looking for qualified staff to meet the demand. It was rumored that the professor who taught the logic class was found working at a shipyard sorting metal bolts into different cans. The one who taught Philosophy just escaped from Germany and left his study of Nietzsche at a German university.

The library space was stretched to its limits. Serious students used the time between classes to study in the great hall with large tables. Students often left their books on the table to go to the class expecting to return immediately to their place at the table. Meanwhile other students were forced to sit at the perimeter using chairs with only a sideboard for writing. It was most uncomfortable. Too many vacant spaces were left unoccupied at the table with only a book to reserve the space. Many such places were left unused four hours at a stretch. Students like Chester after waiting for four hours began to ease their book aside and used the space they left. Common courtesy for serious students was to refrain from conversation while at these tables. Unfortunately too many freshmen, especially young ladies chit chat for prolong periods of time. More than once, Chester told such persons to do their visiting downstairs. One such culprit turned out to be the daughter of the President of the University. Chester felt no regret for educating the young ladies, regardless of their pedigree.

Sunday evening was always church time. During the second year of study at U.B.C., he aspired to sing in one of the church choirs. He liked the music they sang and the high vaulted ceiling was especially appealing to Chester. It was the church in which the Baccalaureate Service for the university was held. He met the choir director who invited him to the chapel. He opened the hymn book and started playing the piano. He asks Chester to sing the bass part of the hymn. Chester didn't do so well. That was the end of the story, but not quite. Many years later, after his Master degree in Social work, he was invited to candidate for the Associate Minister position to start of counseling center for the community. For many reasons he declined.

During his sophomore year, Chester had a "'born again experience" under a religious group. True to his character, he threw himself completely into their activities. He attended their Bible study group every morning before classes, and even became the editor of their newsletter. He became friendly with one of the young ladies. Before too long, Chester was taken aside and advised by the secretary of the group that he did not want to see him fraternizing with the women in the group. It was quite shocking to hear such statement from an employee of the organization, representing the official position of the group. That was in the 40's, and the attitude was very conservative. There was no doubt that a line was drawn in the sand over which one must not cross and such friendship was considered a taboo.

Chester took classes in Chemistry. He loved the lab experience and did very well in qualitative and quantitative analysis. He even had dreams of becoming a chemist with a master's degree. Racism and discrimination against minority race was very much in the forefront of young students mind. The general feeling of exclusionary posture was very much an important issue to consider in finding employment. This became a concern for Chester as he thought of his career. This issue became so real that he felt prompted to ask his instructor, Mrs. Johnson, "What is the probability of finding employment as a chemist if I graduated with a master's degree in Chemistry?" Though she answered affirmatively, Chester still pondered whether it was true in the real world. Was the world ready for such a step forward?

There were many cultural events to enjoy on the campus. Vancouver Symphony held their dress rehearsals twice a year at the auditorium to which students may attend free of charge. That was a great opportunity to be introduced to a wide range of classical music. Along with that, there is the music club in which students could eat their lunch listening to classical music from a superb sound system. These were the fringe benefits of going to a place of higher learning.

By taking a general arts curriculum to include physics as well as philosophy, Chester was able to be trained as a Meteorologic Officer with the Department of Transport later on. That opened another option for him in his career choice.

~

# Chapter 9

## Saskatchewan winter

What Chester learned about Saskatchewan winter during high school days did not prepare him for the winter in the north country of Saskatoon, 400 miles up north.  In Moose Jaw, the locality is considered urban with houses to break the wind.  At St. Andrew's College, it was 400 miles closer to the Arctic circle.  The countryside was flat and did not offer any break, and the wind had a clean sweep across the country.  Early after his arrival to Saskatoon, he was given some advice by his two roommates about winter survival.  One could expect to have 40 degree below zero as the norm for winter season.  One can also expect 60 degree below zero temperature for at least two weeks when the cold arctic air blanketed the region. Those were the time when one must exercise care not to expose your skin to the wind for any length of time and ran the risk of being frost bitten.

There were seven bridges across the South Saskatchewan River within the city limit.  There was one that was very close to the university.  One should find the midpoint called the "point of no return."  If you find yourself unable cross that bridge in its entirety, make sure you turned back before this point of no return.  If you were caught in the open and there was a stiff wind blowing across the river, it would be a very serious situation for your health.  During the winter time, traffic will always stop in deference to the pedestrians.  They always have the right of way, because they are exposed to the elements while the driver was protected inside the cab of the vehicle with a heater. That was why drivers in the prairie were generally very courteous and more patient than at other places. When the wind was blowing with snow on the ground, a blizzard was formed, very similar to a white out situation. Wind can carry the snow without any obstructions to form mounts across highways that was higher than two story building. To deal with such condition, the highway department used rotary plow with huge rotating blades in front of the truck to make way for a Greyhound bus to go through. In such weather, unless you had a definite reason to go outside such as going to classes, you stayed indoor and kept warm. For the first time in his life, he saw street cars using coal burning stove to heat the inside of the vehicle. When the streetcar got to the end of the run, the conductor would leave his seat and stoke up the heater with coal to produce heat for the passengers. It is an unusual sight to see a tiny chimney on top of the street car with smoke coming out.

Many of the married students left their family and came to the city to attend classes. They would return home for the week end to preach the Sunday service. Meanwhile their cars would be parked outside for three days and nights without being used. When the weekend came it was necessary to use a shovel to get live coal from the furnace and put it under the car's engine to thaw out the oil in the oil pan before it would start. No one complained because that was the accepted part of life in the winter.

Everyone at the dorm was young and energetic and the winter never stopped them from doing anything that is normal. Sunday worship went on without cancellation, young people gathered for the weekly activities and meeting without interruption. People took it in stride but always provided themselves with safety margins in their activities. In the midst of winter, everyone learned to enjoy life and find the wonders of nature to keep sane and happy. Every night, there was the northern light to delight their senses and who wondered how colors were mixed among the waves of light in the sky. When you were walking in the hard packed snow on the sidewalk, you learned to note each step you take and listen for the crispy crunch beneath your feet. There was always different sports to engage in during winter, playing ice hockey, ice skating with your friends, and curling using a forty five pound granite stone down the lane. For more affluent people who could afford to travel to the slope of the mountain, there was skiing and slalom to challenge them. There were always movies among the five theaters to choose from, not to mention the book clubs and dinner parties that you could organize.

One learned to dress properly during the winter. Subzero temperature that was dry from the arctic felt invigorating if you were appropriately dressed. You learned to wear clothing in layers with a wind breaker at the outside. You learned to wear overshoes to provide insulation between your shoe and the frozen snow. Older persons learned to conserve body heat by wearing a layer of soft suede next to their skin. One must learn to throw fashion to the wind and cover your head for the largest amount of body heat would leave the body at the head. Law enforcement personnel, who must be outside, often wear bear skin to protect themselves with insulated underwear. One respected the winter condition and paid good attention how to protect oneself from frost bites and over exposure to the wind.

For farmers, they often used horse drawn open flatbed sleds for transportation. Many times, the driver would just stand on the sleigh to carry hay to feed their animals in the field. Frequently they made short cuts over back yards where the snow drifts would be higher than the fences. One must be very careful to watch for the metal clothes lines which were just about the eye level of the driver. Many accidents have been reported when the frozen metal clothesline burns into their eyes, resulting in blindness.

~

# Chapter 10

# St Andrew's College

After his undergraduate study, he attended St. Andrew's College to study Theology in preparation for ordination to the ministry of the United Church of Canada. Although he was in Saskatchewan during the last two years of high school, Saskatoon was five hours road time north of Moose Jaw and the wintry temperature seemed much colder during winter. Thirty and forty below temperature was the norm during winter and sixty degree sub-zero temperature came every year and stayed for at least two weeks.. One learned to stay indoor unless one must go outside between classes. He lived in the dorm and classes were held downstairs. Nevertheless, one developed a healthy respect for frostbitten ears and toes. The native sons called it invigorating and compensated by quickened steps and wrapped their mouth and nose with warm scarves and ear-muffs.        One special treat during these cold nights, was to watch the northern lights in the sky.  They danced and swayed in technicolor like waves in the ocean surf to entertain us mortals, leaving us with wonder and awe, "who would be so ingenious to provide such spectacles for our enjoyment?"  He spent much time marveling at the beauty of His handiwork, as he remembered the hymn, "declare the hand that made us is divine."

He shared the dorm room with two other students during his first year in residence.  Dave was his classmate. while Steve was a pre-log (pre-Theology)

A highlight of the year was to go to the summer field as a student pastor to gain some experience in conducting public worship and in preaching.  The learning gained during the short interval of twelve weeks was extremely rewarding, giving students some idea of what to expect after ordination.  His roommate Dave did not do so well.

"And how did you like going to the summer field, Dave?"

"Not so well.  It was horrible.  There was nothing to do, nobody to talk to and I was all by myself."

"Did you not meet anyone whom you like among your parishioners?"

"Yes, I met them all.  They were very nice and polite and all that, but no one can talk to me at my level.  All they care about is the weather, "is there enough rain for their crops?""

"What else did they talk about?"

"They talked about their children and how they are doing in the city. If I heard it once, I heard their stories a hundred times before."

"Didn't you find someone who is interested in the things you like, such as sports, fishing, hunting, skiing, or things like that?"

"Actually I didn't. I am interested in literature and reading the classics and very few of them went beyond high school. You know how it is, when they talk about carbonation and gear ratio and power take off they can talk your ears off. They never heard of Plato or Socrates."

"What kind of concerns do they have in life?"

"Their biggest worry is that hail will flatten their crop . They can remember to the day, when the hail storm hit them and wipe out one third of their crop. They remember the dust bowl days when the wind blew days and days on end. They hope that will never happen again."

"I am sorry that you had such a poor time last summer. Perhaps next summer will be different."

"I doubt very much if there will be next summer. I feel like a fish out of water in the country. I was brought up in the city like Windsor, Ontario. There is always something to do, you never get bored. As a matter of fact, I am thinking of withdrawing my candidacy for ordination in the church. The work is not challenging for me..."

"What brought you to think of the ministry in the first place?"

"I had this world shaking experience with Jesus. It was such a life changing event for me, it gives me new meaning in my life. You can even say, I had a love affair with Jesus and found my destiny, and that is to share this joy with others."

"Did you see such opportunities in the field?"

"If it is there, I didn't see it. Everyone was so engrossed in their little world, they hardly have time to eat or sleep. Some farmers farmed six sections or more. During busy time in planting and harvesting, they kept their three tractors going, 24/7. When their wives brought their meals to them, the women folk climbed on the tractor to keep them going. They didn't have time to sleep, when they came to church, as soon as they were seated, they dozed off to sleep. I tell you the world has lost its mooring and everybody is chasing after the almighty dollars."

"Don't you think that is exactly the reason why they need to hear your message?"

"Yes but life is too short and it is too uncomfortable for me to work under these situations. I have a lot of thinking to do and I hope that my teachers can help me sort out some of the things that are bothering me."

He was a good student in the classroom, in many ways brilliant in scholarship, had a good command of Greek and Hebrew, but he lacked the skill or interest to relate to people and could not relax himself in the presence of strangers. He found that he was much too introverted to interact with parishioners and did not enjoy the rural life of a farming community. He had many interviews with the professors and the principal of the college but he moved out of the dormitory at the end of the third semester. He found himself a job, doing drafting for a construction company. Eventually he got married and started a family. The last he heard about Dave, he was very happy in his work. Blessings on him and his family..

During the second year, Chester had a new roommate, Howard Groom. He was "Howie" to everyone in the dorm. Howie was very special and became Chester's role model. He was trim and tall, very suitable to be an athlete or a marathon runner. Always clean shaven, impeccably dressed with shining shoes and neck tie, though not stuffy like an Englishman walking with an umbrella and wearing a bowler hat, he represented integrity and self confidence to this young adolescent seeking to develop his own identity. Howie was an extremely bright person, focused, balanced with a good sense of humor. He knew why he was in St. A. and knew what were his goals in life. After spending thirteen years working as a linotype operator in a Toronto newspaper company, he resolved to study for the ministry. He was already married with a young daughter. It must have been a gut wrenching decision for him and his wife to pick up the family and to come to Saskatchewan. He was settled in Hanley, Saskatchewan to serve a small congregation while he commuted sixty miles to study at the University of Saskatchewan. It was a difficult adjustment for his wife Edith to be left alone with a young child from Monday to Thursday each week and to fend for herself. Nevertheless, she knew why they were there; for Howie to get an education. They adapted and prevailed over each new demand of living in a strange land and hostile climates. They were the heroes whose gutsiness made Canada great.

Everybody on the top floor knew Howie. He was the first one to rise in the morning to do his morning routine. He had one of these self sharpening razor which needs honing to keep its edges sharp. The blade rode in a cradle over the wet stone, as it rocked back and forth, it rattled like a volcano and the thundering sound reverberated in the tiled floor bathroom which could be heard down the hall. It served as the alarm clock for everyone at six o'clock each morning. Though it was jarring to the ears, it motivated late sleepers to "rise and shine" and be ready for breakfast at 7:30 each morning.

It was one fall evening shortly after the semester had started that Chester took an evening walk around the neighborhood when he heard the wailing sound of the bagpipe playing in the distance. Like a bloodhound following the scent of the quarry, Chester followed the squeal of the Hebrides and located the source. He knocked on the door and inquired if he could speak to the piper. His name is Malcolm who came to the door and greeted Chester with a jolly "Hello." They soon shared their mutual interest in the bagpipes.

"Do you belong to a band?"

"Oh yes, we practiced every Sunday afternoon in the Legion Hall. I am sure the pipe-major be glad to talk to anyone who is interested in bagpipe music."

"That would be super"

"What time shall I come?"

"I leave here at 1:00 pm"

"I will be here."

"His name is McPherson. I am sure he would like to meet you. What is your name?"

"My name is Chester. See you Sunday."

That Sunday Chester met Pipe-Major McPhee who started him playing on the practice chanter doing the scale. He taught Chester the correct way of fingering and playing the grace notes. He was a good teacher and a good mentor in music. Chester did his homework well and progress as far as he could without a set a pipes.

There were several weeks between the end of the formal study at the college and the meeting of annual conference at which time, suitable candidates were examined and recommended for ordination to the ministry. It was supposed to be very thorough and intimidating, to be questioned by ten strangers on almost anything they wished, everything and anything from your personal life to your theology on your view of the Rapture and the second coming of Christ. To his surprise, there only one question asked of him and a hypothetical one at that.

"Suppose there is a man in your congregation who gradually drifted from his faith to a point where he no longer believed in God and wanted nothing to do with the church or religion. What can you do for him and how would you approach him?"

Chester knew it was a trick question. Regardless of his response, he knew they would countered with a dozen negatives, and said, "That has been tried and it did not work." He decided to cut to the chase and answered with the following.

"I assume that he had been counseled by experts and qualified people. In such case, I will pray for him and rely on the work of the Holy Spirit to minister to him."

Chester felt that he was guided to give the most adequate answer possible. The ordination took place at his home church from which he was a candidate. It was a happy occasion for everyone, including his high school principal who gave him the guidance counseling interview six years ago. "All's well that ends well."

~

# Chapter 11

## Kisbey Saskatchewan

What a thrill it was to score your first goal. You felt like a child who learned to balance himself on the bicycle by finding the center of gravity, "Look, mom, no hands!"

Chester would never forget Kisbey because so many firsts in his life took place there. It was there he learned how to build a fire in the wood stove and kept the fire going in the furnace overnight. Although they had a wood stove in the kitchen at home at Moose Jaw, seldom he had to start a fire from scratch. By trial and error, he learned to place the kindling in a certain position on top of the newspaper, light it with a match and attend to it, careful not to overload it but allow the air to circulate. Local natives told him how some of his predecessors with less experience, just emptied the coal bucket into the fire box, threw a match in and expected it to light like a propane gas stove. There was no hot water tank beside the stove, and each cup of hot tea would have to start from scratch. The pace of life was much slower then, none of this hub-hub scheduling. The most difficult thing to master when living by yourself was with the furnace, to learn how to bank the coal for the night and leave just the right amount of ventilation in the fire box. Many times there were minor explosions and the door of the furnace flew open when everything was just perfect for spontaneous combustion. Without exception, it always happened when he was in a deep sleep.

To Chester, every town conjured up little things in his memory. Kisbey has its artesian well. You could have excellent drinking water by driving a sand point to the ground, even right beside your kitchen sink. To his knowledge, Kisbey was one of the few places where this was possible. Kisbey was the name of the first white man who saw buffalo in Canada. He was honored whenever the call letter for the radio system, CBC in the province of Saskatchewan is used. It is called "CBK." "K" stood for Kisbey, so these were the local colors for Kisbey.

There was an old barn behind the parsonage. It has seen better days. It was ready to fall down on its own. The resourceful parishioners thought that they can salvage enough material to build a one car garage for the new preacher. Mr. Reed, a man in his eighties, volunteered to do the job. Everyday, promptly at eight in the morning, he would be at his post. Little by little, he worked by himself. At 10 o'clock in the morning, Chester always served him morning tea.

"It is 10 o'clock and time for tea. Come in and have a rest."

"I think I will. I enjoy the break, my bones creak along telling me to have the oil change. I am not as strong as I used to be."

When Chester felt that the tea was steeped enough, he always used the best china available and served him using cup and saucer. Chester gently put it in front of him along with a spoon expecting him to help himself with the sugar. This ritual would always take place, Mr. Reed would take the spoon and tap the cup twice and said, " I never drink my tea hot. That is the reason why my stomach is in better shape today than the day when I first got it from my mother." With that, he would push the cup and saucer twelve inches from the edge of the table. He would proceed to tell what he accomplished so far and what was the plan for the rest of the day. After his brief report, then he would take his cup of tea with both hands to drink it down all without a break. Immediately, I would fill his cup again, and he would repeat his mantra, "I never drink my tea hot. That is the reason my stomach is in better shape today than the day I first got it from my mother." Chester was always amused at this ritual. As long as he was happy, why should anyone care. He was a good worker; eventually Chester would be getting a new garage for his car.

The people in the country were among the best in the land. They maintained the traditional value of caring for each other. He felt a special bond with them for there was no pretense in their behaviors. Since Kisbey was such a small community, probably they knew each other when they were babies and many of them had baby sat for each other.

"Are you too busy today to go ice fishing with a friend, Rev.? By the way, my name is Sheldon, what is yours?

"My name is Chester. Glad to meet you. Never too busy to spend times with my friend. What do you have in mind?"

"There is this little lake not far from here where I had my ice fishing shelter right on the ice. Its a lot of fun if you have not yet been initiated to fishing through the ice. What do you say if I meet you here in 30 minutes. Make a thermos of tea or coffee and we'll get some bait on the way and let's try our luck."

"Sounds like a good idea. I look forward to it. See you in 30 minutes, Sheldon."

At the edge of town, they stopped at a convenience store and bought some bait. Then they drove along a trail through some trees for a quarter of a mile after they left town. The snow left a cover so the dips on the road were not seen. What was a quarter of a mile seemed like a giant dipper in an amusement park. Finally they arrived out in the open and a small lake with eight or ten huts spread out in front of them.

"Here we are. The air is nice and fresh and there is no wind. That helps, for the shelter is not exactly wind-proofed," Sheldon said.

He drove the car right up to what looked like an overgrown outhouse with a little stove pipe on top. The car slid to a halt. Chester unloaded the gear while Sheldon played with the combination lock on the door of the shelter. When he opened the door, there was a stale odor of coal oil rushing toward them. He could see a bench against each side of the wall. At the far end, there was a square table with a couple of gallon cans on it and a metal pie plate underneath. On the floor, there was a round hole measuring about eighteen inches. Everything was dark inside and the only source of light came from the door so narrow they have to turn sideways to get in. Sheldon quickly took the can of coal oil they brought with them and filled the can left from last year. It had a small hole through which the oil dripped to the pie plate. Sheldon took his lighter and lit the vapor of the evaporated oil and they have an instant fireplace. Meanwhile they got all their gear inside and closed the narrow door. Everything was dark except for the small flame from the corner and the hole in the ice between the two benches.

"Oh, I can see the bottom of the lake. There are fish swimming around looking for food. This is fun. We shall come here often."

"I'll give you the combination to the lock and you can come here anytime you want. I have spend many afternoons here by myself and just enjoy the quiet time. Sometime I hear the loons in the distance, sometime it is just so quiet I can hear my own heart beat."

"I can tell you right now I am going to enjoy this afternoon. Let's get our worms on the hook and see if the fish will come to see us."

"We are not going to catch any fish unless our line is in the water."

Deftly he took a worm and hooked it through and dropped it in the water.

"Here, let me show you my favorite way to hook the worm. It is the easiest way to do it. It never fails to get the fish."

With both lines in the water, each poured a cup of coffee for themselves and settled down for the afternoon. By now the heat from the makeshift stove supplied enough heat they had to take off their outer wind breaker.

"And how do you like our little town of Kisbey?"

"I think it is just the place to be. I came from the city but I always feel more at home without the crowds and the constant noise of traffic. I like the people best of all, they are all so friendly and helpful. I appreciate all the new friends I made, both in the church and even total strangers."

"That is very good. I heard many good reports about your work so far, and I hope you will stay with us for a long time."

"And are you married, do you have family?"

"I am divorced from my wife three years ago. We just didn't get along together. I like the outdoor and she likes in indoor more. Little disagreements between us became huge issues and we just couldn't see eye to eye on too many things. And winter is too long a time to be cooped up together when there is no place to be by yourself to get your own perspective in place. We parted as good friends, I still keep in touch with her, she is still a very nice lady."

"I am sorry things didn't work out between you two. But did you have any children?"

"We are lucky that way. We didn't have any children. Just the two of us. That made everything so simple when we decided to part ways."

"And what do you do for a living?"

"I was lucky at the stock market. I bought enough shares of Kodak when they just started out and after it got going and it split many times, I am able to enjoy myself and just live off the coupons. I was just lucky."

"I am glad for you. Do you have any hobby to occupy your time?"

"I like wood carving. I specialize in wildlife. You should come to my house, I have a good collection of duck decoys. They are very authentic with the right colors. I also carve caricatures of animals. It is a great outlet for my energy. I could make them as ugly as I want when I am feel ugly inside or as funny looking when I feel happy and on top of the world. Everyone has different moods at different times. I have so many around, I give them away to the children in the hospitals when I go to the city."

"Do you like hunting, Rev.?"

"I never had the chance to see if I like it or not."

"I do my hunting with a camera. I capture some very nice shots of hummingbirds hovering in the air. I develop all my own pictures. That is the other half of the fun. I hope you will come to see my studio."

"I have done very little in developing my own pictures, just enough to see what the process is like. So far, I have been busy studying, trying to do all my assignments on time."

"Where did you go to school?"

"After three years with U.B.C., I went to a little college called St. Andrew's in Sakatoon and spend three years with them. It was a small school with only four professors. Each one double up in their teaching load. My New Testament professor taught church history as well. He was a very good Greek scholar from Edinburgh. He was an expert in form criticism......There I see a fish checking out my worm. I never saw one like that ever before...That is exquisite.."

Sheldon moved closer to the hole and had a closer look at the fish.

"That is a keeper....Just let him play with it for a little while before you set the hook.....Now ..yank hard....you got him," as he noticed the wiggling of the tip of the fishing pole. "Don't reel him in yet, let him tire himself a bit, have some fun with him....Now is a good time, reel him in, Rev., and when you get close to the surface, the last motion is the most important one. With one motion, pull him out of the water without hitting the floor board."

Chester followed his instruction and lo and behold, it was a northern pike measuring twenty inches.

"I did it, the first fish I caught in my life and it is a keeper, too. All thanks to you, Sheldon for coaching me; you are a good master fisherman."

"Good job, Rev., you're not only a fisher of men but a real fisherman for sure."

"Just open the door and throw the fish out, it will be frozen by the time we are ready to leave."

Just at that moment, Sheldon got a bite and immediately he reeled him in and it was an eighteen inch Northern pike also. As he threw it out the door, he said,

"What say you if we have some music to celebrate." He took out his portable player from his backpack and turned it on. To my surprise it was bagpipe music.

"I hope you don't mind this kind of music, I was brought up with it and gradually I developed a taste for it. Now, I can never have enough of it, it reminds me of home in Glasgow."

"How lucky can it get. I happen to like bagpipe music very much. I dreamt that someday, I learn to play that instrument myself. Did you say your home is in Glasgow? How did you land in Canada and in Kisbey?"

"I was in the Royal Navy for twenty one years. When I resigned my commission, I met this lovely lady in Halifax, fell in love and got married. Kisbey was her home and she brought me here and I stayed ever since."

"Did you "see the world" as the saying goes?"

"Yes indeed, I travelled around the world twice. I saw the Far East and India. Spent a lot of time in Singapore. I'd like to settle down there. The food was wonderful and the climate just suited me fine. But I fell in love with a Canadian lady and she was from Kisbey and here I am."

"I came from Hong Kong myself. I have some great memories about the place. But Canada is a good place to be. Lots of wide open space and lots of opportunities for anyone who wants to work hard."

"That is what attracted me to stay in Saskatchewan. So much open space and fresh air, plenty of it."

"Do you mind the cold weather, when it gets down to twenty below?"

"You learn to adapt. When the weather is too cold, there are lots of things to do and stay warm. That is when I took up wood carving."

"I like your attitude. I suppose you learned that in the Navy; you learned to adapt to all sorts of situations when you are out at sea. It is just you and the open water when you are on watch."

"Do you ever get lonely here in a small place like Kisbey?"

"Never, I feel I am always in touch with my friends all over the world through my ham radio. Just last night, I was talking to my friend Domenic in Auckland, New Zealand. The night before, I talked to my friend Dugan in Cairo, Egypt. He is the manager of a trading company with fourteen camel trains. He was born just two street from our house in Glasgow. We never met each other until we stopped over in Cairo many years ago. How can anyone be lonely when you can talk to your friends all over the word? I have friends in Chicago and in Florida and keep touch with them regularly. My ex couldn't care less. She is very content with knitting her baby blankets for her nieces and nephews. To me, that is too tame. How about you, do you have any hobby?"

"I couldn't say that I have. So far, I have buried my nose in books for the last seven years. There are many things I like to do, that will come later on.

After I read the biography of Sonja Haney, the Olympic figure skater, I took up figure skating while I was in high school. Sorry to say, I haven't skated for ten years. I should take that up again. It is good exercise for your whole body......Oh, I think I got another one on the line..."

Sure enough, he hooked another keeper on the line. Before the afternoon was over, between the two of them, they landed seven good sized fish, not a bad day's catch. It was getting dark and they began to think of home. The temperature began to drop and it was getting to be quite chilly. They doused the fire, packed their gear and their catch and drove home.

That certainly was a good day; caught enough fish for two days and met a good friend. After that outing, they became good buddies and they spent many evenings together, sharing their love of the water and the latest first hand weather report from all over the world, from Sweden to South America, from Los Angeles to Lampora India. Life in Kisbey couldn't be any better.

One afternoon, Chester made a house call to a young family out in the country. When he knocked on the door, a three year old girl open the door. Immediately she turned around and called out to her mother in the kitchen.

"Mom, the Rev is here. And he is a handsome man."

"I am Rev. Louie, and what is your name?" he asked the little girl while they waited for her mother.

"My name is Abigail. And I am three years old."

"Hello, how nice to see you," said her mother. "Do come in and make yourself at home. Abigail couldn't stop talking about the new preacher when she came back from Sunday School last Sunday."

"She is such a smart girl and to have that vocabulary for three year old. You must have spent a lot of time with her. Do you have other children or she is the only one?"

"I like to have a little brother to play with," interrupted Abigail into the conversation.

"It will be a while before we have another child. There is so much to do on the farm to get started, it took all my energy to keep up with things. How do you like Kisbey so far? The people are so friendly around here. I came from Toronto myself, the big city and it took me a while to get used to living on a farm. My husband is very helpful and my in-laws are just so precious. I feel like I am part of the countryside now. Away from the crowds of people. Now I have a chance to sit down and catch my breathe periodically. Do you come from a big city yourself?"

"I grew up in a big city like Vancouver in British Columbia. I am like you, I prefer the quiet pace in the country. There are lots of things to do, it really depends on yourself to find things that you enjoy doing. eIs this a big farm that you and your husband manage?"

"We are taking over Dustin's father's farm. It has been in the family for five generations and we are doing our best to keep it in good shape. Perhaps you like to see for yourself and have Dustin show you around a bit."

She turned to Abigail and said, "Go to the barn and tell Daddy to come in. Rev. Louie is here to see us."

"OK Mommy," Abigail skipped off by herself.

"I was told that the McLean's farm is one of the larger ones in this area. It isn't enough to own seven sections but that you rented five more sections from your neighbor to put crops on. That must keep everybody very busy. How many tractors do you keep going?"

"We can't do it all, there is enough work to keep five workers busy besides Dustin and his dad. During harvest, we keep three combines going twenty four hours a day until the crop is harvested. Beside, Dustin likes to keep cattle and compete in the Royal Winter's Fair in Toronto each year. That was his passion. After he graduated from Quelph, he was lucky to take the championship in breeding Jersey milking cows. He was the champion for three straight years. He is well known in the industry. So between his cows and the twelve sections of crop to manage, we don't have much spare time to ourselves.....Here is Dustin. Hello honey, Rev. Louie is here . We were talking about your hobby of breeding Jersey cattle. Maybe you would like to take him to your barn and show him your pride and joy, Daisy."

"Glad to see you on our farm. If you don't mind the dirt and being around animals, come to the barn with me and I will be glad to show you around."

They left his wife at the kitchen and they headed to the barn with Abigail close behind her daddy.

"Can I feed my little calf, daddy?" and she turn to me and said, "She is only six months old. She is all mine, I saw her when she is born and I fed her every day. I want to raise her all by myself. I call her Pinball."

The barn was at least five hundred feet long. The cement floor was kept clean with mechanical equipment and lots of water.

"I see the floor is clean, how do you keep it so spotless?"

"I made a huge septic tank outside and wash all the waste down through a trough into the tank under ground. Through a system of weeping tiles, the liquid is drained away throughout the field. What you see in front of you is the milking parlor of my own design. The animals are fed as they are being milked. Everything is done mechanically and no hands ever touch the milk. Once a day in the morning a tanker truck comes and empty our storage tank and bring it to the depot for processing."

"How many cows do you milk a day?"

"Around two hundred, give or take a few either way. Beside that, we try to keep the herd going by having twenty new calves at any one time. It keeps us very busy. At harvest time, we have to keep our machine running day and night."

"How do you manage to keep everything running smoothly?"

"That's where I come in. I sit on top of everything. Sometimes we get into a tight spot and even I have to climb on the tractor myself. When things get hectic, we couldn't even take time out to eat dinner."

"What happens then?"

"We get our spouse to keep the tractor running while we climb off to have a bite to eat. The only time we stop is to fill our gas tank."

"We all work very hard, this farm supports seven families. Last year we had a bumper crop and netted a decent sum. We try to give a little more to the church but we put a large amount back to add new equipment and a new barn. You have to keep up with things, or else they fall down on you. Have you ever worked on a farm? We might just call on you some day and have you drive a truck for us."

"That sounds like fun. Yes, I've worked on a farm once, two of us boys tried to put a prefab granary together without using any nails at all. It took us most of the summer to finish the project. I even tried to milk a cow, only I didn't know any better. I tried to milk her still wearing my work gloves. The joke was on me."

"That would be hard to do, unless you are an expert."

"Daddy, can we go and feed Pinball now?" Abigail asked.

"It is about that time isn't it? You go ahead and get things ready for her."

Abigail went happily off to find a bucket and fill it with a special mixture from a bin. She went ahead to find Pinball. As soon as Abigail appeared at the gate of the enclosure, Pinball came to meet her. The calf just snuggle up to her and rub her chin against her chest and nearly pushed her over.

"Of course, I try to do all the repair in-house and it keeps me very busy. There is always something that gets broken. I am just thankful I can do most of the work myself, else it would cost us a pretty penny."

"I heard that you won the Championship in breeding division at the Royal Fair in Toronto. That must have been quite an honor. You are competing among the cream of the crop."

"That was quite exciting. I gave the rest a run for their money. I think I was just lucky. But to do it for three years, that is different. I must have learned something from my genetic class at Quelph. The thrill is over, now I go just to have a break during the winter and give my wife a chance to shop in the big city like Toronto. She seemed to like the outing."

"Thank you very much for showing me around. I hope the Lord will bless you again this year and give your family good health. How is your dad?"

"He seemed to be able to keep running like an old clock. Sometimes I feel that he still can run circles around me. He is in very good shape, for a man in his late sixties. I hope I have his amount of energy when I get to his age. Drop by anytime, always glad to see you. Our door is never locked; you are always welcome at our table. I better get back to work, the cows are getting very uncomfortable at this time of the day. They want to be fed also. Good bye for now."

I left them with a good feeling. Here is a young man, a good husband and a good father, a good manager in his business and very successful in what he is doing. And there are many young men like him in my congregation, hard working folk and generous supporters of the church. With that kind of folks on the farm, Saskatchewan deserves the name, "the bread basket of Canada."

Winter time was to be taken seriously. Always travel with warm blanket and a day's supply of food and water, for anything could happen on the road. Snow blizzards were common and lethal. Special care must be taken to maintain your car to tip-top shape. People installed special heating elements embedded in one of the bolts that hold the head to the main engine block. One of the routines of Saturday night for Chester was to plug in this engine block heater. The first thing he did on Sunday morning was to activate the heating element, so that the engine would warm up so the car would fire up. Unless your battery is fully charged, even the warm heating block could not help you.  On one occasion, he had to resort to ask his friend to help with transportation.  There were many who were generous with their time and effort, always ready to make this newbie feel comfortable in his new home.

People in the farming community had a special kinship for each other that was not found in the city.  It was easy to be yourself because the person who sat next to you had probably changed your diapers when they baby sat for your mother.

Life was an open book and everyone knew everyone's business by the telephone party line.  One Sunday morning, the worship in Farmede was set to 11:00 AM.  As usual, Chester always started promptly in order to end on time.  Housewives might have a roast cooking in the oven and it would be poor taste to have the service run over for thirty minutes.  That particular Sunday, the service started without the organist, singing the old familiar hymn,"The church's one foundation....."  At the third line, a young lady and her aunt entered the church.  Lois with her white wide brim hat proceeded up the aisle, found the page in the hymnal, came up to the platform and started to play the reed organ, blending in with the singing before the beginning of the second verse.  She continued until the end of the hymn and acted as if nothing happened.  Such was the informality and close knit atmosphere of the country church.  Lois and Chester became good friends after that, she was a teacher at the local schoolhouse and became a social worker with her master's degree from Edmonton.

There was a lady, who acted most kindly toward him.  Although she was brought up a Roman Catholic, she supported his church and many times she called him

"Father." She was most attentive to his needs, many times she invited him to join her and her husband at her dinner table. Occasionally, after the evening service was over, she would have some of her friends to have tea and evening snacks together. It was a welcome change to be able to relax a bit after conducting three services on Sunday.

Daily routine for a bachelor clergy in Kisbey was simple enough. It was not a chore for him to devote the morning to study at the dining room table, had lunch and made pastoral calls in the afternoons. Evenings after supper were free time for reading and visiting friends of his choice. They included friends like Bill Burgess who was the pastor of the neighboring church ten miles away, or the high school principal two doors down the street. When a snow blizzard made walking outside a test of wisdom, and forced people to stay indoors, he developed a liking to knitting and crocheting. He even knitted an eight inch square dolly and gave it to the women of the missionary group to be auctioned off to contribute to their cash box. Everyone thought that was an unusual article to have on their shelf.

The other church in Kisbey was an Episcopal congregation, with a rector in charge. Obviously he was directly from England because he had a very strong Yorkshire accent. He spoke of his home in England and they compared notes of their childhood. He was an avid fisherman and an English soccer fan. Those were the days before television, otherwise he would be able to see England on TV and not limited to listening to BBC radio reports. He had an even smaller congregation than Chester and he can imagine how isolated he must have felt beside just talking to his wife. He wished they had become better friends but he was never available to socialize with each other.

Summer time is for camping outdoor. There is a church camp sponsored by the United Church at Carlyle Lake. The first summer he was in Kisbey, he was invited to be one of the leaders. Without ever been to camp himself, he thought it would be a good place to have some new experience. The most aggravating thing about camping as a group was the morning dip. It was unreasonable to expect young kids to get out of their warm bed and be immediately plunged into the cold lake water like blanching vegetable. It was commonly accepted as a part of camping life and no one complained too much about this inhumane treatment of our young people. There were crafts to enjoy, outings to new places to visit, places they had never heard of. It was a great experience to be among thirty active boys, who were not above playing practical jokes on the leader if he were not two steps ahead them.

Next town to Kisbey is a small town called "Forget." Unless you are initiated, you are likely to pronounce it the way it was spelled. Chester learned quickly, it was once a French settlement and the name was pronounced like "Forshay." They invited Chester to have his fourth service there. Since it was not through proper channels, he had no choice but to decline their invitation.

It was while he was in Kisbey that he ordered his first new car. He was driving an old Pontiac with a bad ball bearing at the rear right wheel. It soon got from bad to worst and he was forced to get a more reliable car. There is a provision made by the Home Mission Board for anyone receiving minimum salary, for a loan of one thousand dollars, interest free to buy a new car. This is a once in a life time offer.  One hundred dollars will be deducted monthly at source.  With such an arrangement and the courtesy of his superintendent driving it from Oshawa Ontario to Saskatchewan, he was able to save on the delivery charge.  This made it possible for him to have a more reliable means of transportation on Sunday.  He was so proud of the car that he washed it every week, whether it needed it or not.  That was a Plymouth and served him well for many years.

Within three months after he took delivery of a new car, he had his first accident.  He was driving to the first morning service, when a dog streaked full tilt from a house toward his car.  "I paid him no mind and just minding my own business."  All of a sudden, he heard a banging noise from the right side of his car.  He did not know if he had run over the dog.  He must have spent just a second too long looking at the rear view mirror for a dead or live dog that he found he had slid off the road and was heading toward the ditch.  At that moment, he had the choice to pull the steering wheel sharply to the left for correction, running the risk of losing control of the car and ended up in a slough on the left side of the road or just let the car continue on its path.  He had the presence of mind not to take the risk of overturning the car, and he just let it slide into the slough on the right side of the road.  The water leaked in slowly and covered the floor board of the car.  To exit the car, he had to lower the driver's window, and climbed out unceremoniously like a thief. Meanwhile whatever had been on the front seat slide on to the floor and was found floating on the water.  The owner of the dog witnessed the whole affair and offered to help.  He told her of his destination, and she suggested that she calls ahead to someone in his congregation to come to rescue him and the car with a tractor and chain. In due time, the garage checked out if any damage had been done. After the carpet of the car was dried out, life continued. Chester can assure you, the party line was busy for a whole day and possibly for a whole week about the latest encounter of the preacher with a dog.

The highlight of the year for any prairie town is the "fowl supper." It is an affair highly anticipated by the caterers, usually it is a church group, after the combining of the crop has been done. A typical family would donate and volunteer to cook a turkey or to bake two pies. Some would give twenty pounds of potato or carrots or other vegetables. On the day of the announced dinner, ladies of the church would start working in the kitchen in the early afternoon .

"Jean, would you mind if you start to shred the cabbage and carrots and make the salad for us?" Martha, the coordinator of the group would gently suggest and to assign jobs to individuals.

"Right away, I'll get it started," Jean replied.

"Rose and Lily, would you two mind to set up the tables and chairs. Mr. Turner will give you a hand if the table is too heavy for you to manage. He is in the furnace room waiting to help. Just give him a holler if you need his help."

"Jenny, it would be a great help if you can rinse the silverware and make them nice and shiny. You know how it is, some of the ladies are particularly critical to look for such details. I am sure you will do a good job."

Toward 4:30 in the afternoon, more ladies appear at the scene bringing in food, with an apron ready to lend a hand. Soon the kitchen is full of workers and everyone was busy with their tasks. The kitchen was beginning to be filled with fragrance of roasting turkey, ham and roast pork. The fragrance of herbs filled the whole dining area. The tables were covered with white paper and Thanksgiving decorations which made it colorful and cheerful. Rose and Lily did a super job to provide the proper festive ambiance to the whole area. There are casual conversations among them though the kitchen was filled with activities. It looked like a manufacturing facility as the basement was being set up for the first sitting at 5.30 pm. Men and children visited and socialized on the church ground, while the older folk waited in the sanctuary of the church. Tickets were sold beforehand with the time of serving written on them. Promptly at 5:30 everything was ready, ticket holders came in and they were served family style.

"Everything looked so nice, I really look forward to this supper here at this town," Johnathan remarked to his neighbor.

"Are you out of town coming to our supper?"

"Yes, we come from Arcola, fifteen miles away. Our daughter married a farmer outside of town and she always get two tickets for us every year. We come to visit her and the grandchildren and try to make a day of it."

"And what is your daughter's name?"

"She is Mrs. James Cooper."

"Of course, I know Alice very well. We live just two miles from her. Our children play with hers and they ride the school bus together....Did you have the big downpour of rain yesterday? I heard some farmers got rain out and many roads were flooded."

"Yes, we had the same rain. Fortunately almost everyone finished their combining and the grain was safely in the grainery."

"Here, are you ready for the turkey? Here is a good piece for you."

"Thank you, don't mind if I do. I like the drumsticks the best. They seem to have the best flavor."

Further down near the other end of the long table, another conversation took place.

"And how is our neighbor doing today?"

"Just fine. It seems we have been so busy the last few weeks combining that we hardly see each other lately."

"Harvest time is a busy time for all of us, hurrying to get all the work done before the weather turns on us. I tell you, before long, we can expect to see snow and winter will set in. Now we can take it easy a little bit. Although there are many things to do, to catch up on things that had been neglected during harvest time."

"It seems ironic to have fowl suppers every year. We always want to do our share, to support the church and all. Every year it is the same thing. We donate the stuff, my wife cooks and prepare the stuff. Spent the whole week planning for it. Bring them to the basement of the church and then turn around and pay for the whole family to eat the same stuff. It just make better sense to me if we were to give a lump sum to the church and cut out the busy work. That is just my opinion."

"I see what you mean. Some year, I feel the same way. It does make better sense to do your way. It is as if we don't have enough to do around the farm to keep us busy."

"You know the women, they think differently than we do. They say that it is a good time for everyone to socialize a bit. It is good for the children and them to see each other and to work together. It is good to see each other beside sitting in church on Sunday and listen to the preacher. They feel they need to have variety in their life."

"That makes sense. They say, if you have a happy wife, you have a happy family. Do you agree?"

"How true that is. Heck. What is the point of working so hard if it isn't to make your wife happy. If the wife is not happy, no one is happy. I found that out a long time ago. Here, have some salad. It is the kind you like, if I remember correctly."

"Don't mind if I do. Everyone needs some roughage in his diet to keep you regular. Otherwise you feel constipated, especially sitting on the tractor all day."

"And are you expecting to go to Toronto for the Winter's Ag Fair?"

"I expect so. It is a good break for both of us, she like to go shopping in the city and I like to submit an animal in the milking division. My animal took second prize last year. This year, I like to do better because I have changed her diet by using different formula."

"Good luck to you. I might bump into you up there at the fair."

"I hope we do. We can have lunch together, the four of us. That will be fun."

And so the conversations among men and children could be heard. After the last meal was served, everyone crowds into the sanctuary upstairs to enjoy the entertainment, a talent show organized by the organist. Joseph E always plays his version of the Silent Night on his accordion, while Sarah sings a soprano solo of "Bless this house." Chester got into the spirit of things and sang a solo, "Old man river" with black face paint. He received a standing ovation for his effort.

People in a small town like Kisbey had traditional values and still believed in bartering. One time, Chester had a surplus of potatoes given to him and he decided to share it with a needy farmer. Very soon, there was a tractor, pulling a trailer full of small branches and a mobile saw drawn up at the yard. The farmer was busy sawing the wood into kindling length and throwing them down to the basement. Chester had enough kindling for a whole year. Such was the way the folk "look after their own".

~

# Chapter 12

## A seed that change his life.

Within two weeks of Chester's arrival to Kisbey, there was a knock on his door.

"Come in, please. It must be 2 degree below zero out there."

"It is a bit chilly. My name is Connie and he is my fiance, Bill."

"Glad to meet you both. Here have a seat."

"We come to ask you if you can marry us on Nov. 1st ?"

"As far as I know, I am free that afternoon. What time do you have in mind?"

"You name the time and we will be here."

"How about 2 p.m."

"We like a very quiet affair. Just us two and two witnesses. Can we have it right here?"

"I don't see why not."

"You know I just got here and this is going to be my first ceremony as far as a wedding is concerned. Now if I lose my place or make a mistake, you know why."

"That's alright, Rev. If you got stuck, we'll prompt you because this is my fourth time and this is his third time at it."

"Does it mean that you were widowed three times and he for two times?"

"Yes, unfortunately, that was the case. We are lucky to have found each other. This time, we want it to last for many years."

"I am sorry to hear about your past misfortunes, but I rejoice with you in your new adventure together this time. Certainly I will tie the knot tightly this time so that it will last a long time."

"I am certain you will do your part."

"Make sure you have your state license with you that day. Without it, we cannot do anything."

"We know all the ropes, after all, we have lots of experience. Is there anything else, Rev.....If not we will see you Nov 1st, 2 p.m."

"Ok, we'll see you then. Blessings on your both."

Everything went off without a hitch and everyone enjoyed themselves that day. A red letter day for them but an extra big red letter day for Chester for he conducted his first marriage ceremony successfully.

But the story did not end there. It haunted Chester to no end. He asked himself many times since then, "what could he have said to help them on their way?" He felt awkward about the generation gap, that they were of the age of his grandparents, with so many more years of life than he. They must gone through more pains and joy than he could imagined. As the Chinese would have said, "They ate more salt than I could have dreamt of." Here he was, still wet behind his ears, just a freshly minted newbie, still trying to find his own footing, What could Chester have said to contribute to their future happiness? He was clueless about the subject of premarital counseling. He felt a void in this area of training and preparation in the helping process. Gradually Chester developed a dream for the future, to speak effectively about truths that were important toward a successful marriage. Reflecting back, that was the seed that changed his career goals for the rest of his life.

~

# Chapter 13

## Among Lords and Earls

"And do you know that Beatrice is pregnant and she is expecting the baby in August?" Katie's sound carried itself across the churchyard right to the parsonage.

"This will be her third child." Lizie's answer was heard between the squeaks of the only water pump in town.

"What about Mrs. Watts? How is she feeling during the last three days after her surgery in Regina General?"

"She had her daughter from Swift Current to stay with her. Amy is so nice to come from all that distance, especially when she has her own family of two boys at home. I suppose you do what you have to do. Reliable help is so hard to get these day."

"How is your son getting along with his new bride? They are married two and a half months by now. I wonder when are they going to make you a grandmother?"

"I hope they will take their time at this, especially when both of them are working. Do you know what "DINK" stands for?

"I have no idea"

"Double Income, No Kids."

"They are trying to save enough money for a down payment for a house in the city. Everything is so expensive these days. Young people expect to start out with everything new. When you and I got married, we make do with what we had. Just got out of the depression years, we were just beginning to pull out of the slump."

"There, I am finished. I got the pump all primed up for you and you are ready to go. Oh dear, it is ten o'clock already. I better get going before I miss my favorite show on the TV, 'The Lawrence Welk Show' .....Why, here comes your neighbor Maud....I will leave you to her....Good night.....Hello Maud...I got to run, see you."

So from the kitchen of the parsonage, Chester can hear the conversations of everyone at the pump especially at night when the wintry air was calm and everything was as peaceful as walking on a deserted road in the open country. When all you can hear is the cricket chirping and his mate answering back lovingly.. Chester could hear about all the latest news around town, the updated reports of recovering patients from the hospital, the exotic cruise to the Panama or the Bermuda, or the food served at the latest wedding reception. Some were vicious, equal to any character assassination on record, others were funny as a two headed clown. It provided endless entertainment if he cared to listen to women indulging in their favorite sport beside tapping in to the telephone party line..

When Chester first heard of Earl Grey, he had mixed feelings about moving from all the friends in Kisbey. When they started to tell him about the parsonage, being only nine years old and equipped with running water, he was very anxious to hear more. When they informed him that it is only forty five miles away from Regina, he was definitely interested because his fiance was finishing her nursing training in Regina General Hospital. It meant that he was able to cut down the driving time to less than an hour to see her. After the on site inspection of the parsonage, they arranged for the formality of notifying the conference authority of the intended change of "pastoral relation" between the two churches.

Earl Grey is definitely the bedroom suburb of Regina city among the rich gumbo soil farm land, of Saskatchewan. There is no industry in this small town of under 2,000. Most of the professionals commute to the city, while the rest of the residences are "suitcase farmers." The school children are bussed out of town. There is a train station in town, post office, a grocery shop with a hardware section on a one block main street. There is one garage around the corner. The two churches, a Lutheran and the United Church completed the tourist attractions of Earl Grey.

The parsonage was a modern stucco bungalow with one bedroom and a full basement. The running water was provided from a reservoir tank in the attic. It was filled with rain water pumped from a cistern at the basement. During dry season, the local "dray-man" was hired to deliver surface water from some "slough" from a field. The drinking water is supplied from the one pump behind the church. The floor plan of this house was wide open, without any partition except the bedroom and the bathroom. The furnace was expected to heat the whole house including the basement. During winter with outside temperature of 40 degrees sub zero, coupled with a blizzard blowing outside, the snow begins to creep in from the outside door, the house becomes a cooler. The possibility of separating the main floor from the basement was proposed, but the parsonage committee could not come to any unanimous agreement, so the proposal was tabled. But there was one family who understood the unique problem. He proceeded to build a temporary partition on his own, he paid for the material out of his own pocket. Apparently for him, it is easier to ask for "forgiveness" than to ask for "permission". With the partition in place, the main floor was adequately heated by keeping the kitchen stove heated 24/7 without having to fire up the furnace.

It was customary for Chester's father's congregation in Moose Jaw to have its Christmas concert on the day after Christmas called Boxing Day. It fell on Chester's shoulder to read the scripture during the celebration. By the fifth year, he was able to recite the narrative from memory. During this brief time, his eyes wandered and noticed a young lady playing the piano. She wore a yellow chiffon dress with her hair short cut. Upon further inquiries, she turned out to be the daughter of one of the church members. She was on Christmas vacation from the nursing program from Regina General Hospital. They were introduced to each other and began dating. She lived an exceptional life, she survived through the Japanese occupation in mainland China. During the day, the family would pack enough food and hide in the mountains. They would return for the night and repeat the same routine the following day. Only five years ago, she and her brother left for Hong Kong and Canada before they met. Within two years, starting from scratch to learn English, she mastered the language sufficiently to have graduated from high school and was accepted into the nursing program in the hospital. Beside all that, she was an accomplished pianist, able to play Bach and Mozart. Chester remembered at her capping ceremony, she was honored by her classmates to play a solo piece on the piano "Where e're ye walk." written by Handel. Shortly after that, they were married and Chester brought his new bride to Earl Grey. Everyone instantly fell in love with her. She was a natural at being a minister's wife, outgoing with an engaging smile, and a genuine caring for people. Unfortunately, after three good years of marriage together, she was diagnosed with a brain tumor. After a full radiation procedure, and after remission of ten years. She died after being in a coma for ten weeks. It was an extreme tragedy and a great loss to everyone who knew her.

While Chester was at Earl Grey, television was a novelty. Although it was only black and white, it was a real treat to view the video. He remembered his organist had such a TV set and it was not unusual for her to invite her friends to view programs at her home after the evening service. One of the favorites for them was Ed Sullivan Show. It was quite a sensational moment when Elvis Presley was introduced for the first time. They all felt that his gyration on stage was vulgar and too suggestive to say the least. Little did they know that he started a whole new chapter in American music, the Rock and Roll era. Another feature on TV was the wrestling shows between the heavyweights. Many of the wrestling icons have long disappeared from the scene except Hulk Hogan. The organist's husband and Chester would get so involved and excited that they would groan and moan like children when the wrestler were thrown into the air, and landed, shaking the whole platform. It was reported by many that they emerged from the show afterwards, hand in hand, as they headed to the nearest pub for a drink and a good meal together. It was much more realistic if they continued to believe that they were fighting like gladiators in the Roman coliseum. Those were carefree days, when life was simple and innocent.

~

# Chapter 14

## Life as a Salty Sailor

Although the minimum salary for pastor was only one hundred dollars a month, the customary way to pay him was to give him the money from the weekly collection plate and make up the deficit at the end of the year. More often than not, the weekly collection amount to less than twenty five dollars. There was no way for Chester to set up any budget and maintain the household without using credits from the grocery store. It was time to think of an alternative in terms of career.

The first summer at Earl Grey, he joined the Royal Canadian Naval Reserve List as a Chaplain. The purpose was to find a supplement to his income and also to explore if there were career opportunities for him.

Chester and his wife drove cross country to the west coast with a three month old baby. What a thrill it was to smell the saltwater of the Pacific Ocean again. The drive across half of Canada, was as boring as brushing your teeth until they crossed the Rocky Mountains. There were miles and miles of flat land in Saskatchewan and Alberta. They were as flat as a pancake, only punctuated every nine miles with a solitary grain elevators beside the road. Though the Trans Canada Highway was straight like an arrow, one must stay alert for there were still hazards to avoid and small animals like groundhogs that insisted on bisecting the path of the vehicle at the wrong moment. Crossing the Rockies was an experience never to be forgotten. They witnessed the endless row of snow capped mountain peaks jutting against the cloudless turquoise sky and saw the Fraser River, thousands of feet below. It was an unforgettable sight to see cars on the road below them, with their headlights on during the evening. They appeared as specks on a ribbon threading through the darkness. Though Chester had crossed the Rockies thirteen times by airplane and train, it was a humbling experience to travel by car through the mountain range and to remember that years ago, thousands of Chinese immigrants invested themselves with sweats and tears in labor to build the Canadian Pacific Railway through these mountain range.

Another reason for going with the summer program of the chaplaincy service was to find out whether a military career was in Chester's future. After the exposure to problems common to the families of sea faring men, he came to the conclusion that the naval career was not for him because the prolong sea time was not conducive to his family life.

The reason why Chester chose the naval service over other branches as a possibility was the long tradition it had. It is considered the senior service in the military and therefore marches at the head of any military parade. Whoever is the commanding officer of the naval establishment and often it is a Commodore, his family always attends Sunday worship, and he always reads the lesson in Sunday worship. In fact, the Chaplain receives a salute from him once each morning as a courtesy and recognition of his office.

The place of Chaplaincy service has a long tradition in the British and Canadian Navy. At every shore establishment, promptly at 8.00 am, the bugle sounds, and the color is raised. But prior to that, morning prayer is said by the chaplain. He is allowed three minutes to say his piece. Woe to him if he runs over the allotted time, the raising of the color will be delayed and he is apt to have a friendly chat with the commanding officer later on that day about keeping this naval tradition of precision timing. The shortest prayer on record was that of Lord Nelson, "Don't forget us when we forget you, Lord. Amen."

There are other naval traditions that are time honored. In the Officers' Mess at the dining table, there is always an empty chair left for the Engine Room Officer. Woe to anyone who breaks that rule.

Whenever a "man of war" is under sail, each "rating" is entitled to a ration of "grog" to settle their stomach and to combat sea sickness. It is a mixture of hard liquor and water. This mixture cannot be stored overnight because of the presence of water. Those who are underage was given the equivalent amount in currency and credited to his account. The Petty Officers, who lived apart from the ordinary seamen, have the privilege of mixing the liquor with coke to add more fizz. Chester, being new on the cruise and needed more visibility was given the supervision of issuing the daily ration, his job was to make sure that the grog which is left over each day is dumped overboard.

For the second summer that Chester volunteered his service, he was assigned to HMCS Iroquois, a destroy escort, as the relief chaplain. He joined the ship at Quebec. The ship was on a flag waving cruise to visit Three River as a reward to the city since they sold the largest amount of saving bonds at a recent competition. It was an exciting experience for Chester to board a real naval vessel under sail.

It is a tradition that the Chaplain does not wear his rank on his sleeve, though he receives the equivalent pay as a full Lieutenant, (a Major in the Army). This allowed him to enter the ratings quarters and he ate with them at their table. It must have raised eyebrows among the officers to see this chaplain to behave in this manner.

There was an outstanding incidence that Chester will never forget. During one of the stop overs in one of the small cities along the cruise, the ship was docked to entertain the local city officials. They were invited to come aboard and hors d'oeuvres were served. Every officer was ordered to wear their Number 5's (their Sunday best.) and play host. Chester found one who spoke fluent English and carried on a conversation. He was reaching for his cigarette and Chester wanted to light it for him. Because it was quite windy on deck, Chester cupped his hand to protect the flame from being blown out. Unfortunately, Chester had not enough experience with such thing that the rest of the match book caught on fire, causing a minor burn at the inside of his left hand. It was uncomfortable enough to require attention at the local hospital. His left hand was wrapped in bandage with salve and ointment on it. In due time, the bandage was discarded because it was causing too many inquiries from everyone around him. Chester was sure that the captain heard about it, but never a word was said from him. He sent word through his secretary and to pay his compliment and wishes for a speedy recovery.

Word got around that a vessel of the Royal Canadian Navy was docked at the wharf downtown and the Chaplain was invited to be the guest preacher for the Sunday worship. Chester had the privilege of representing the Canadian government and brought greetings to the worshippers that Sunday as he preached from the pulpit. He was greeted warmly by the congregation at the reception afterwards.

Just before the departure from that city, one of the officers returned to the ship in an unusual way. He was delivered by a piper cub airplane using the length of the wharf as the runway. All activities on board ship halted to witness this unusual landing. Excitement was building up as the miniature plane circled above to survey the prospect of the landing stripe. No one had ever witness such a daring feat. At last, the plane committed itself to landing and made the approach. Everyone held their breath. Many crossed themselves while others just silently stood and stared. Finally,the plane landed and came to a stop just feet away from the building. All joined in to give a spontaneous applause and gave a sigh of relief for a job well done. The suspense was not completely over. Everyone knew that the pilot must leave the wharf successfully before the job was done. The suspense began once again. If the pilot had the skill to land within this limitation, there was a good chance that he would be able to take off using the same distance. The small plane turned around, the engine roared to full throttle, reminiscent of a take off from an aircraft carrier, and lurched forward and was airborne. That was a remarkable demonstration of the pilot's skill and judgement. Many wondered if the pilot had not been a naval combat veteran, quite familiar in judging distance and had nerves of steel in his belly.

Chester also had the privilege of working alongside of the navigator as the ship "sail" toward the Gulf of St. Lawrence. He was using visual landmarks along the river banks. Chester knew for the first time what the phrase 'by hook or by crook' meant. It referred to the light houses from which mariners get their bearings before satellites and electronics navigational aids.

He also was able to witness the history of the early settlers in the days of Chaplain and Jacque Cartier. Early settlers were given land along the St. Lawrence River. But the land was in a form of a long narrow strip at right angles to the river. Each parcel had water frontage. From the vantage point of the river looking landward, it was very colorful to witness the division of land holdings. They appeared like a quiltwork layout along the shore line. Chester could easily imagine himself to be the fishermen returning with their catch in the boat and counting the strips in order to locate his own homestead.

Chester also witnessed the landscape of Newfoundland. All one can see was trees and nothing but trees. The ship touched port at Cornerbrook and was given a royal welcome by the local dignitaries. The local chaplain entertained Chester by taking him fishing for a day. The trout was running very well and they netted a good day's quota, sufficient for a cookout for the host's family. The ship returned to Halifax and Chester took a plane back to Ottawa to start his training with the Department of Transport at Carlton College.

~

# Chapter 15

## Touch Down in Ontario

After serving four years in the pastorates, and starting a family, Chester decided to take a two years leave of absence to consolidate his finance and to chart his career goals.  He had not forgotten his first wedding ceremony in Kisbey and the empty feeling of inadequacy.  After proper inquiry, he secured an appointment from the Department of Transport, Canada, Weather Division to be a trainee as a Meteorologic Officer (Met Officer) at Toronto Ontario.  This fulfilled his needs.   Toronto is the center of economic and intellectual activities.  It is the site of the University of Toronto, close to Queens University in Kingston, McGill in Montreal, University of Ottawa and best of all the United States.  Oh yes, the beginning salary for trainee was three times that of what the church was paying him.  After giving due notice to the Pastoral Relation Committees, he packed a small baggage trailer, and reported to Ottawa to begin the Orientation and remedial study of Calculus and Thermodynamic classes at Carlton College.

It was 4 pm. Friday afternoon, Chester found himself in front of the Parliament building in Ottawa, He was caught in the biggest traffic jam in the country.  Four lanes of traffic, each bent on getting out of the city, either going home or to the Gatineau Mountains for the week-end.  Here was this country boy, who had never driven in a city during any rush hour, now he was confronted with this new situation.  There was no choice but to be sucked along like in a whirlpool in a kitchen sink.  Fortunately the five month old baby was asleep in his mother's arms in the back seat. Finally the nightmare ended and he found his way out of the mess.

He found the correct address of the old mansion house in a conservative neighborhood. He fished for the key in the letterbox as instructed by the owner who had gone to their summer home for the season. The heavy oak door creaked open and they were greeted with a cavernous hallway half the size of the house they left in Saskatchewan. The chandelier hung from the ceiling showing the carpet well worn by the traffic of tricycles of the children and grandchildren who came to visit them. All the furniture in the house was sturdily made like it was meant to last through many generations. There were elaborate cupboards on the wall in the kitchen, and one would expect a tapestry in the dining room. In its place, he saw an old portrait of a highlander with a shield at his side and a broadsword in his hands. There was no doubt as to his noble birth.

As Chester unpacked his tiny baggage trailer that he dragged all the way from Saskatchewan, he inspected the cartons that contained his wife's treasured sewing machine, to make sure that no damage was done. Then he gingerly opened the cartons with his Hi-Fi sound system, his pride and joy that he put together from a Heath Kit. Everything seemed to have survived the rugged cross country Canadian route, skirting the barren and rocky northern edge of Lake Superior and bypassing all the big cities like Sudbury and Toronto along the way. After the crib was set up for the baby, it was time to prepare supper and to eat at the dining room table. It was a massive piece of furniture, fit for the banquet hall of a castle. There was only one thing out of place. these antique chairs were on casters. The plates available were stoneware and the utensils were heavy as lead. They were made to last.

The study was equipped with a humongous oak desk, suitable to honor the signing of the Magna Carta. All that Chester needed was a little desk to do his assignments from the Calculus and Thermodynamic classes. Throughout the Calculus class, he had the strange experience of a pre-existing life for him. He was sure that he had come across these problems before, although he had forgotten the solution to them. It was long afterward he found out that indeed he had taken this Calculus class seven years ago during his undergraduate study. It was really Thermodynamics that he lacked, but the Director of Research decided that he might as well take Calculus as a review class to refresh his memories.

There were only three students in the class of Thermodynamics. After the third lecture, one dropped out and only the two of them were left in this seminar. The classes were treated very informally, the three of them would sit around in his class room quite casually as if we were having a friendly chat among old friends. The professor was a theoretical physicist, who obviously was more at home with more esoteric topics like electrical fusion and high speed frequency radio transmission than teaching the two students entropy, viscosity and laminar flow of liquids. He would come to class wearing flip-flops and a crumpled Hawaiian shirt, with three "mastiffs" trailing behind him. These animals came in only two sizes, huge, and super sized. They had the frame of a miniature donkey and reached the belt of a normal sized man. Dr. Debian would lean back in his chair, until one day he fell backward. The students tried to keep a straight face in his presence, but afterward during coffee breaks, they fondly reminded each other that that was how relaxed they would become if there were too much Physics in their brain. Now when Chester had time to digest the material five years after the fact, the subject boiled down to this simple idea. Each contributing factor to the entropy would be represented by a fraction (in terms of how many tenths) of the attribute in the total equation of calculation. At least that was the principle taught in that class. He passed the class after writing a supplemental exam on the subject, three months after the class was dismissed.

The schedule was full from 8-5 in the classroom. After a brief nap, it was suppertime, played with the baby briefly, and it was study time from 7pm to 3am. He slept from 4 to 7 am, breakfasted at 7.30 and then he was off to classes. He kept up that schedule for the summer. He never worked so hard in his life. He knew he had to make it, it was a matter of a "do or die" situation with him, because so much was at stake.

Just before Chester was ready to leave Ottawa to return to Toronto for the second phase of the training, the owner of the house, Donald McPhee and his wife dropped in to do their laundry. Chester was relaxing on the couch listening to Bach's music.

"What kind of savage music is that you are playing on the gramophone?"

"That is Bach, my favorite composer."

"What did you say was this fellow's name?"

"Bach. He was a German, who composed music for the pipe organ. Bach."

"Never heard of him. What a strange name, Bach. Couldn't be very famous because I haven't come across him among my books.  Give me a rousing march on a wee set of pipes or a strathspey, played in quick time and I'll dance to it any day.  But this organ business sounds like a baby winning for milk, it is too tame for me."

"So you like the bagpipe music, eh!  I happen to like bagpipe music myself.  Sorry I didn't bring any with me, we came from Saskatchewan with a small baggage trailer.  There is only so much room and the baby's crib and other equipment takes priority.  You know about all that.  Where are your children now?"

"They are in Australia and London England.  One is an attorney, he became a barrister and practiced in London.  My other son is an artist. He decided he likes the desert in Australia.  My daughters are all married with children and they live around Kingston and Halifax."

""How many grandchildren do you have?"

"Altogether, the last count was ten, and two great grandchildren."

"What sort of work did you retired from, Sir?"

"I was a land surveyor by training.  I did most of the work around the Maritimes.  Have you ever been to the Maritime?"

"I just returned from a cruise with the Royal Canadian Navy, HMCS Iroquois.  We went up the St. Lawrence River to Three Rivers, Quebec and returned by way of Newfoundland."

"What were you doing in the navy?"

"I was a Chaplain on the ship.  I sailed to relieve the regular chaplain for his maternity leave while his wife was having their second child."

"Do you ever see combat?"

"No, I did not go overseas. Besides, I am only on the Reserve list."

"That is a switch, a Chinaman in the Canadian Navy. I never heard of such a thing before."

"Oh yes, there is a Captain in the Canadian Navy and he is a Chinese, at least an Asian. Must be quite a sight. He could have been easily mistaken as Admiral Yamamoto of the Japanese Navy, couldn't he?"

"Oh yes, don't get me started on Japan. We should gas everyone of them. Such cowardly attack on Pearl Harbor!"

"Didn't they say, 'All's fair in love and war?'"

"I don't know about that. When I fought with the Scot's Guard in WWI in Africa, we fought to win. Either we kill or be killed. There was no two ways about it."

"War is terrible."

"I lost a son in the navy. He was on convoy patrol, when his ship was torpedoed by the Germans. He was such a bright lad with such a promising future ahead of him. He was an Electrical Engineer, graduated from Royal Oaks in Esquimalt B.C. Will always be proud of him.....My wife tells me we are ready to go. Our chores are done for this week. Hope you find everything you need. Make yourself at home. We are pleased that we can help you out while you are studying at Carlton University."

"We are indebted to you for such wonderful accommodation. It is such a splendid house, built like a castle in Scotland. It is a joy for us."

Mr. McPhee left behind his charm which brought back fond memories of Ottawa for a long while. Chester packed up his little trailer again and motored to Toronto to begin his second phase of training with the Department of Transport to become a Met Officer.

Toronto was such a big city compared to Regina, Saskatchewan. One could easily get lost if there were no cousin to help him. He finally found a second floor apartment with a family on Palmerston St. just six blocks from the office and the classrooms at the University of Toronto. It was small, but adequate for his needs. It was very close to Chinatown where his wife loved to shop for groceries. The family downstairs came from Europe with two young boys, age nine and twelve.

"And where did you come from?" ask the landlord in belabored English.

"We just came from Ottawa, but we were from Saskatchewan before that."

"And what brought you to Toronto?"

"I am going to start a new career, I hope. I am going to be trained as a Meteorologic Officer or a weather forecaster."

"Where can you get that kind of training?"

"The Department of Transport has an office on Bloor St. They will do the training at the university next door."

"Come on up and see if the apartment would be big enough for you."

He, his wife and the baby followed the landlord upstairs. There was a large room at the front facing to the street, behind that is a dining room, and then there was a kitchen, a little small but big enough for them.

"What do you think?"

Chester looked at his wife and she nodded approvingly.

"The rent is sixty dollars a month and the electric is included, right?"   "That would be fine, we will take it."

"Agreed.  When would you like to move in?"

"Right now, if it is alright with you.  We will prorate the rent for this month, at the end of this month.  Is that O K with you?"

"That is fine with me.  Let's shake on it."

They shook hands on the deal and Chester went downstair to unpack his tiny trailer.  They decided to make the front room to be their bedroom and arranged a little makeshift desk at one corner.  That way, he could study late and just jump right into bed.

Chester's focus was to have a place to study in a quiet atmosphere.  Typical of growing boys (ten and twelve years old) being confined to the house, their energy level was quite high and they made the normal amount of noise.  So studying time for Chester was after everyone had gone to bed.

There was an electric stove with an oven in the kitchen that came with the apartment.  That Christmas, they decided to have baked ham to celebrate the season.  He put the meat in a roasting pan and put it in the 400 degree oven.  Soon there were smoke from the oven and it spread to the rest of the house.  Fortunately, there was no need to call the fire department, since they caught the situation before it went out of control.  What was needed was to open all the windows to air out the smoke and put some water at the bottom of the roasting pan.  With a glaze of honey and mustard and cloves, the stage was set for a good meal.  The baked ham turned out to be a success.  He even took half of it downstairs to his landlord as a peace offering.

Candidates who responded to the recruiting for Met Officers came from a variety of backgrounds. All had earned their bachelor's degree at universities. At least three of them majored in Mathematics, five with a degree in Physics. One was employed as an assistant in a gunnery range in the military. Several were teachers, all had a background or some knowledge of Math and Physics. Although Chester had basic courses in Math, Physics and Chemistry, he was the only one not working in a field related to Science. There were three young ladies in a class of twenty seven. All students appeared to have come from the middle class, quite bright and intelligent, each was quite comfortable wearing shirt and tie in the summer weather.

The class room material was very interesting. In the morning, lectures dealt with the characteristics of different air masses, the general terrain of the North American continent, and the location of large bodies of inland lakes and their modifying effect on the weather. The afternoon lab was devoted to the understanding of the weather maps. First they learned how to plot the information on the map, then how to read it quickly and interpret the maps. Using it to forecast the weather did not come until the last phase of integration of all that they learned. It was interesting as well as challenging to analyze and determine where the fronts appeared on the map. It required detail understanding of all the information presented to you from the map. Some students managed quite well, others lacked the mind set to pay attention to details and thought only in broad general terms. On one occasion, a student turned in an exercise with the front drawn in a straight line from the Gulf of Mexico to the North Pole. Obviously he failed the exercise for that afternoon. The mistake was serious enough to prompt his withdrawal from the program. The art is to digest the information in totality, which was more than the sum of its parts. It was a joy to hear an expert explain why the front was put at a certain location because the clue was found in just one small piece of information on the map. Such analysis was done by the professionals who won their master's degree in Physics. To Chester that was the only creative part of forecasting. The time he spent studying at night appreciating the finer points of placing the fronts from old maps paid off handsomely. The daily progress of the student was carefully monitored. It was expected that the survival rate in the class is less than 50%. Through hard work and studying, Chester survived the course to this point and the staff gave him an overall grade of "third class honor." Chester was familiar with first and second class honor to reward outstanding students for their extra ability, but third class honor was something new to him. He was sure there were more than himself to puzzle over such title. Of course, they could do anything they wished in the academia. He accepted it as their recognition for his persistent effort to do his best.

For the second phase of the training, it took place in an air force base in Trenton, Ontario. It is the place where pilots made their transition from propeller driven planes to jet power engines. The training involved the Met. Officer giving a live weather briefing to the pilots before take off.

At this time, the Met Service was being restructured due to the advent of close circuit TV and other technology. It was undetermined at that point of time what was the future functions of the Met Officers or what role they were expected to play in the service. What plans they had made, the students were not privy to the information. The creative part of the work was done by those with a master's degree in Physics. They would be stationed in the Main Montreal Office. It was rumored that the department would be setting up satellite offices at airports across Canada manned by Met Officers, the para-professionals. The forecasting would originate from Montreal, transmitted via close circuit TV and the Met Officers would fine tune the forecast according to local terrain. In regard to their initial assignments, Chester's greatest fear was to go to a frontier post like Churchill or Hudson's Bay or Yukon or at one of their radiosonde stations. That would be like jumping from the frying pan into the fire. After Trenton, the class returned to Toronto for the last phase of training.

Chester struggled with his future in the department during the last phase at Toronto. The answer came when the church in Tweed, Ontario was looking for a minister. Mr. Way was dispatched by the search committee to Toronto to interview him. He caught him during the lunch time and after a brief conversation, they arranged for a Sunday when he could appear in Tweed to preach for a call. He still remembered one of the questions asked by Mr. Way, "What is the least you will take to accept a call from Tweed." Chester was so glad to have a chance to preach in a church in Ontario, it prompted him to say, "Whatever was the going rate for a church with your membership number." Mr. Way was a used car salesman, and that was the usual bartering approach in negotiating for the price of a used car to be turned in for a new one. That was the only approach he knew. At any rate that was the best answer Chester could have given him. Chester and his family arrived at Tweed and stayed for four years where their second child Denise was born in Belleville General Hospital.

~

Grandma's apartment address

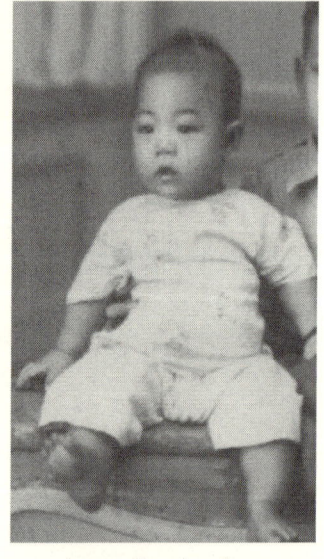

Learning to sit

High school days

Undergraduate days

Recognize me?

End or beginning?

Relaxing in Boston

Free to be me

# Chapter 16

## Tweed, vacation land.

As you walk down the main street of Tweed, you felt like you could expect to see Andy Griffith with Barney behind him. Tweed gave you that sort of atmosphere, laid back, leisurely, quaint and down to earth. The town was nicely laid out as on a piece of graph paper. The streets were clearly labeled with street signs. The bank sat on Main street at the middle of the town. This was the days before plastic credit cards and all business was transacted by cheques or cash. On the opposite side of the street at the far corner was Burnett Grocery store and Thompson's Grocery store at the other end of the block. In between these two stores, there were the car dealership owned by Mr. Way who came to interview Chester in Toronto. Beside him were the Bush furniture. and funeral establishment, a drug store and auto parts store for the farmers. Around the corner of the bank was the Post Office and the United Church. There was the car garage and the grist mill. The real estate office was a self standing small building tucked away and dwarfed by the neighboring office of the Land Registrar.

The joy of being in Tweed was that they had running water, a flush toilet and the good people, not necessarily in that order. In Earl Grey, when the cistern was empty and no water in the reservoir in the attic, they secured water by melting snow from outside. They would fill a 45 gallon drum with snow and melt it down. Disappointingly, it wasn't enough to wash diapers. This was before the days of disposable diapers. Those days were history.

Tweed was a town of six to ten thousand people. It was situated as the launching point to the open country to the north, good for hunting and fishing and summer cottages. The population was divided between the Catholics and Protestants, therefore there were two funeral homes. There were much competition between the two groups but nothing violent. There were three Protestant churches, a Pentecostal group, the United Church and the Salvation Army. Father Baker was the priest for the Catholic church up the hill. The United Church in Tweed was the largest of the three protestant groups. The exterior was made of stone, and inside has a pipe organ.

The musical component of the church was provided by a choir of fifteen to twenty singers. The choir director was the elementary school principal, Mr. Connor. The organist played honky tonk on Saturday night and switched over to play at the pipe organ on Sunday morning. He was a marvelous player and they were fortunate to have him play on Sunday while he farmed on his land during the rest of the week. The Sunday School staff was most faithful in leading classes and the midweek group for girls was led by a capable team of women. One of the creative part of worship was to tell a children's story. The adults enjoyed it as much as the children. Often he took the liberty to indulge in some dramatics, to try to add some humor and entertainment to the congregation, otherwise an hour long service was too hard to concentrate.

An atmosphere of conservatism prevailed the region and Tweed was included. "If it works, don't change it." The front door of the church in Tweed was locked from the inside with a broom handle placed crosswise at the doors.

Tweed was located with its back door to the north country, famous for the tourist trade, for hunting and fishing. Tourists from Toronto and Ottawa came to this area to build cottages to escape the summer heat. A few live there all year round in their winterized homes. Most of the land was owned by the Crown and it was possible to buy it rather cheaply, a dollar a foot of water frontage. Usually a lot was approximately one acre. One can have the title to the land provided one put a building on it with a minimum square footage within two years. Chester liked the area well enough that he wanted to put down some roots. So he went to hang coke bottles at each border of the intended lot at the shore line of a quiet cove. In due time, the lot was approved and he got a permit to put a building on the lot after he paid the Department of Forestry one hundred and seventy five dollars. He secured a used field office, with walls and roof broken down in twenty foot sections. Chester and Pa Elliott built a floor measuring 20 X 40 feet. Mr. Way literally conscripted the men of the church to donate Labor Day to help put up the walls and the roof of the cottage. He promised them that he and his wife would provide a hearty lunch of beef stew and dumplings, with fresh fruit for dessert. Fifteen men turned up and managed to close in the structure at the end of the day. Everyone seemed to enjoy working together with Mr. Way bossing the job. Families of the congregation were very accommodating to empty their garage and provided enough furnishings to make the cottage very comfortable. One family donated their old bathroom sink, toilet set, oil lamps and curtains while others help to build cupboards for the kitchen. There were beds and bunks for the children and they even got plastic pipes for the sewage system. At the end, a total of nineteen Thompson oil lamps were gathered. Someone offered the use of his old outboard motor, while Mr. Way gave him his flat bottom boat stored in his barn for the last three years. Everyone seem to be in a generous mood to help, perhaps it was because Chester had a very opposite personality compared to his predecessor, whom they nicknamed "10% Waterman." Enough said.

No tales related to the cottage would be complete without mentioning the name of Mr. Clarke Rawson. He was a member of the Actinolite Church, one of his "outside" congregations. He stood six feet with a country gentry bearing. He always appeared wearing a bow tie. Though he never wore any headgear, it would be most fitting to imagine him sporting a black bowler hat. That would fit his personality to a tee. He was always clean shaven except for a little patch of mustache above his upper lip. He and Chester met every Monday afternoon and spent the time to put a few nails on the sidings around the cottage. As they leisurely went about the task, which was secondary. their primary agenda was just to enjoy each other's company and the fresh air.

Mr. Rawson spent his career in education, being the principal of the junior high school in Toronto. Before his retirement, he started to build a summer home in Actinolite area. Gradually he winterized the building and made it into a permanent home with a flag pole in his front yard. It was his signature gesture, whenever you see a Union Jack fluttering in the breeze, it meant that he was "in residence".

He had many tales to tell about his career reaching back to the First World War. He was a mule driver for the army, dragging cannons all over France and Belgium. He witnessed the poison gas used in the war and many of his comrades succumbed under this dispicable acts. Clarke was fortunate to escape unscathed.

Just before his retirement, Canadian nationalism began to surface, and  was taking steps to choose a design for a flag.  There were many debates to the choices of designs and colors.  He didn't care what sort of flag Canada adopted as long as Canada has one that is distinctive.  The public thought that there were too much red color being proposed which would suggest Russian Communism.  He said that Russians have no monopoly on the red color at all. The most important thing was that Canada has a flag of its own.  He got his wish.

Mr. Rawson was a good gardener who knew how to put the right amount of fertilizer to make his crop grow.  He supplied Chester with fresh vegetables throughout the summer.  He was a good friend who can talk intelligently on almost any topics.  Chester enjoyed his intellectual stimulation every Monday when they worked together.

Chester learned many things from Mr. Rawson. They spent much time discussing how idioms from other cultures crept into their everyday usage.  Among the elegant phrases which came from the Irish was to say, "It is a soft day."  When you think about it, it was indeed elegant to express the quiet mist of the morning, or the overcast sky just prior to a rain shower.

He was a good man, good Mason, a good husband and a grandfather, but most of all, good friend to Chester. He considered him to be one of his father surrogates, someone whom he admired and respected, something he did not find in his own father.

Pa Elliott was explaining to him a farmer's life when he arrived on his farm one day.

"This farm had been in the family for five generations. My great great grandfather cut the trees down on this tract of land and with the lumber built this house. It was built solidly with a view to the future generations. The walls had four layers of brick to keep it warm in the winter and cool in the summer.

"Who own the land before him?"

"It was crown land. It belong to the king. We still have the original deed. Let me show you."

His wife produced a parchment with a four inch seal made of beeswax, dangling from the parchment by a piece of ribbon. The writings were written by hand and signed by the governor of Canada.

"You said that he actually cut the trees down and sawed them into timber?"

"With the timber, he built the rest of the house and also some of the furniture."

"He must had a lot of help from his neighbors."

"He had to, he could not have done it alone. That was the way of homesteaders, each helping each others."

"Did he had a big family?"

"Everyone had large family in those days. That is where the manpower came from. Everything was done with horses and long hours of labor at the field. Look at this table, it was made from the wood from the land. At one time, this table would be full of men as they ate their lunch during harvest time."

"That is a large table, but it fits the size of this room. It must hold twelve or more."

"Our family plus the hired help made this quite a busy place. One thing they do enjoy is apple pie for dessert." his wife chimed in.

"Do you have any help or you did it all by yourself?"

"I did it all by myself. You have to do a lot of planning. You get used to doing it after a while."

"We had a lot of good memories around this table," Pa Elliott resumed. "When the children were small, they used to ride their tricycles chasing each other, round and round until they became dizzy. They are all grown up now. They all moved to the city except our son Grant. He was the only boy among four girls. He helps me on the farm."

"What is your chief source of income?"

"We raise crops just to feed the cattle. Our income comes from the sale of our cattle. We don't produce any milk, we keep beef cattle and so far we have done well. We put our girls through school, one became a psychiatrist, another a nurse, and the other two were secretaries. Grant here, is going to be a farmer like me."

"Do you ever go hunting in the fall?"

His wife chipped in, "I wish he wouldn't keep so many guns around here, especially when the children were small. Touch wood, there was no accident all these years. The amount of meat he harvested was not worth the risk. He never listened to me."

"It was a chance to get out with the boys. The five of us maintain a cabin in the north. It was good fishing and hunting place. Later on, I'd like to bring you out there and let you see for yourself."

"Do you do most of the repair on your equipment yourself?

"You have to if you're going to be a farmer. In fact, during the war, it was impossible to buy a tractor. So I made one for myself. Went to a junkyard and got an old tractor from an eighteen wheeler outfit and made one for myself. It had an eighteen gear transmission, plenty of power to do anything I want on the farm. Plenty cheap, the whole thing didn't cost more than three hundred dollars. Now tell me, where can you buy a tractor for three hundred dollars. My neighbors were envious and they wanted me to make one for them. I could have but I know they will come back to me for maintenance and that is a chore. Besides, I have my own work to do. I could have made a little pile of money, but I let that one go."

"When do you start to plant your crop?"

"As soon as spring appears, there are maple trees to attend to. We tapped about two hundred trees to make maple syrup. That takes a lot of energy but there is always a ready market for them. There is always a lot to do, and it takes a lot of energy to run a farm. I don't know if Grant wants to be a farmer. He had his own idea as to what he wanted to do with his life. That is up to him."

"It is time for me to go to make another call. It was nice chatting with you. I never knew that there is so much to farming. You taught me a lot today. Thank you."

"Do come again. We love to have you anytime. Maybe for a meal sometime and taste what a home cooked meal is like."

"I look forward to that. Good bye for now."

That was the beginning of a long friendship with the Elliotts. He sort of took Chester under his wing to introduce him to many things he had not done before. Such things as snow shoeing, trowling for muskies and hunting wolves on his farm. He became another father surrogate.

Pa Elliott was one of the wisest men Chester had come across. He had a very patient manner of teaching without saying a word. An excellent example was the time when Chester had the crazy idea of making a leather jacket from scratch. He was trying to act like the Indians of long ago, of shooting the animal, tanning it and sewing it into a garment. Since Pa Elliott was an avid hunter, he would be the most suitable person to supply him with the skin of the animal when he went hunting. He presented the idea to Pa Elliott and he agreed to save him two deer skins. Soon, he came and delivered the skins, wrapped carefully and properly salted. He thanked him profusely. Meanwhile he was doing some research to study the process of tanning the raw skin into working hide. He was getting nowhere. No one gave him any information nor did anyone discourage him with the bad news that it wasn't as easy as it appeared. After weeks of persistent inquiries, he found that it was an extremely complicated and time consuming process which he neither had the equipment or the know how to do it properly. It was two months after Pa Elliott gave him the skins that he finally admitted that that wasn't something he should tackle. One day, he returned the skins to him and thank him again. He took the skins and put them at the back of his truck without saying a single word. He could have stopped his foolish day dreaming from the start and saved everyone the trouble. He chose to let him learn for himself about the process of tanning. A very patient and wise man.

Pa and Ma Elliott contributed much to their lives in Tweed. They were very special people, understanding, generous, giving, patient and very caring. That was the time when our second child was born and when his wife began to be ill. Ma literally took over the care of their newborn daughter. In fact, Denise played in her kitchen and banged on her pots and pans on the floor while Ma Elliott prepared supper.

Any improvement to the parsonage must be approved by the Official Board of the church. It was a large group of over twenty representatives from every group in the church. It was meant to be a forum where every group can speak to the rest of the church about requests or concerns directly without going through a third person. The need of a downstair toilet in the parsonage was discussed. The idea of a second bathroom in any house was an innovative one and unnecessary one at that time. The idea was shelved. Meanwhile his wife was having medical trouble and it was thought by some that it would be a great help not to have to go to the second floor, especially with two babies in the house. But the biggest problem is that there is no logical place to install one. The notion took a back seat in the agenda of the church. Meanwhile the problem persisted and no action was taken. Finally, Pa Elliott grew frustrated with the board and took action himself. He figured it is simpler to ask for forgiveness than permission. He had one at his own house on the farm. It was located at the landing, going down to the basement, which was seldom used. He proceeded to cut the hole himself, bought the toilet out of his own pocket and went ahead to do the job. He enlisted the service of the plumber, and completed the project. Nobody objected and the matter was forgotten.

Pa Elliot had very fine features, trim and well built. He was very much at home wearing a suit as well as in farmer's overall. To look at him in church, one could easily mistook him to be an attorney or a CEO of a large company. He was a credit to his Masonic Lodge, to his profession and to his church.

# Chapter 17

## Ridgeway, the edge of Canada

Ridgeway was very close to the border of United States. In fact, many of the residents worked in United States. The church was called St. John Memorial United Church in memory of the the defenders against the Fenians who came across the United States border trying to overrun the British colony called Upper Canada. The raiders were driven back by the detachment sent from Toronto and one of the road was called Garrison Road in their honor.

There was no sand beaches at the south shore of Lake Erie. For swimming, Americans came to the north side of Lake Erie to a community call Crystal Beach. It had an amusement park but the transient number of summer residents could not support a permanent community. Ridgeway which bordered Crystal Beach became the shopping center for the area. It was an one stop shopping, complete with hardware stores, drug store, insurance offices, two attorney offices, and even a nursing home right beside the church. Even though there was a substantial Catholic population in Ridgeway, they belonged to the parish of Crystal Beach. There were three doctors in town and a funeral director on the main street. There was a large Post Office with many employees and even a jewelry store in their midst.

The United Church was an one point charge, which meant it was large enough to support a ministry without partnering with other congregations. It even boasted having a gymnasium with basketball court. It was mostly middle class families of shopkeepers, and a few professionals like accountants and engineers. The church accommodated about three hundred with a good size pipe organ. There was a growing number of younger families. When the search committee came to interview Chester, they were all in the thirties. They happened to represent a good cross section of the congregation. They were able to revive some of the activities that once thrived in the church, it includes square dancing, bingo nights, badminton tournaments, and of course to continue the Fowl Supper tradition.

It was unusual to include a gym in the architecture of any church. As part of the new addition, they included a very good size kitchen, plus a large sitting room which the ladies used every Wednesday morning for quilting. Chester usually joined them for 10 o'clock tea, which delighted them to no end. Of course they exploited the gymnasium space to have the Fowl Supper in grand style. The supper was known throughout a wide area, folks from Fort Erie, St. Catherines, Crystal Beach and even from Buffalo N.Y. supported this annual event, and of course it added to the annual cauffers of the ladies who worked so hard. Chester was in the middle of it, helping to carve the turkey and handled many food items. Everyone seemed to enjoy working together.

This level of energy among young people was still very much apparent when Chester arrived to Ridgeway. Word got around that Chester was a fan of wrestling. On the second Saturday after his arrival, four young men of the congregation invited him to go to Buffalo to see a wrestling match. It was quite a temptation since that was the time he usually spent in polishing the sermon delivery for the next morning. But in the face of such friendly gesture on their part, Chester graciously accepted and enjoyed himself immensely. He shall never forget their way of showing their acceptance of his presence in the church. He counted it a great honor to be their guest into their homes.

Chester was given a study in the church and a part time secretary so it was easy to concentrate on sharpening his skill in sermon preparation. The question of marriage counselling continued to haunt him, for there was no material on the subject at that time. In an offhanded way, it was Dr. Thompson, a medical doctor in his congregation, who encouraged him to follow his dream to pursue graduate study. Chester asked him if he received any instructions on counseling in his medical training. He admitted that the extent of such training was limited to half an hour of psychiatry. Casually he just dropped a seed in Chester's thinking, that there were some courses available on the subject if he were serious to follow through. Being so close to United States, he started to think in terms of graduate school. The nearest seminary was located in Rochester, NY. He made inquiries about their curriculum and what they offered. After four and a half years in Ridgeway, he enrolled to Colgate Rochester Divinity School toward his Master of Theology degree. As part of his intern programs, he worked in the Residential Treatment Center with Fred Gargential and Dr. Klein in the Outpatient clinic program.

Among the many friends he made, there was none like Robert Disher, who became another father surrogate. The first time he met him was in his garage. He was working on a template. It looked very much like a sunburst with many sun rays emanating from a central globe like the sun. He invited Chester to guess what he was doing. He kept him engaged in his project for quite a long time until he told him that he was making a template for the interior of his Volkswagen van. It was to fit at the upper right hand rear corner of the van where the sidewall met with the rear panel and the ceiling. It involved the meeting of three plains. He was getting ready to outfit his van for the long trip to British Columbia, to show his wife when he was a young man working as a mining engineer. Since that time, he always tried to present Chester with a trivia question. It always kept their friendship alive and interesting. He was an extremely intelligent man, graduated from Queens University in mining engineering. His first job was with a mining company until his father died, when he came back to Ridgeway to manage the printing shop. Eventually he turned to teaching, and became the principal of the high school. From there he retired and tried to live a quiet life. He stimulated Chester's intellectual side, and encouraged him to take steps toward a graduate degree. He kept a very interesting collection of his inventions in his garage. Among them was a special set of wheels and can be self locking when a force was applied in the opposite direction. There were kites of special designs he worked out to drop a parachute at a certain height. There was a special design for catching a mouse without decapitation. He loved to fill his house with special gadgets to help his wife who had poor eyesight. He delighted in collecting antiques, especially of unusual designs. His house was full of toys which could entertain children hours on end. He had a son who was an architect in Halifax and a daughter who lived in the neighboring town. Chester enjoyed his quiet demeanor but most of all, his high intelligence who knew how to stimulate his mental side of life and he counted him among his best friends and mentor as well..

Rev. Gale was certainly one of his favorite persons in Ridgeway. His brother was a missionary to Korea and he came from a rich religious background. He filled the pulpit until Chester came on the scene in Ridgeway. He was a gentle soul, who was a friend to everyone in the community. He was known not only as a faithful pastor but as a excellent woodworker. His love of wood was well known in the area, for he specialized in violin making. He helped Chester to appreciate the smooth line of each curve in the violin. And he developed a love of woodworking which continued to this day. They enjoyed a deep friendship together. Though they seldom talked about theology, each had a commitment to the same God and a strong desire to serve Him according to their individual gift. He loved making and restoring old furniture. He taught Chester canning, weaving with reeds and presented him an armchair which he restored when Chester left Ridgeway. It was a gift he would always treasure because of the affection they had for each other.

Another good friend Chester had in Ridgeway was Frank Clendening, the funeral director. He was one of the few with whom he could relax and listened to his collection of classical music. They must had something in common since they both served the public and maintaining confidentiality was primary in their work. They never talked about the third person in their conversation. He enlightened Chester as to the many aspects of being a funeral director and an embalmer. Some of his experience was quite humorous. There was no way for him to know how long the funeral service would be. He thought that he and his assistant would have time to catch a quick cup of coffee. When they returned to the church, the preacher and the pall bearers appeared through the front door of the church, ready to open the back door of the hearse. Much to his embarrassment, he never left his station after that incidence. They both laughed about it for a long time.

In his career in the ministry, Chester had the good fortune and honor to pass on his apostolic succession three times. Mr. Reid had declared himself a candidate of ordination when Chester arrived to Ridgeway. He was a serious young man who studied at Queens University and the Divinity School there. He finished his coursework after Chester left Ridgeway, nevertheless he invited him to return to Canada to participate in his ordination service. Chester was sure that he was a credit to his family, to his church and would be fruitful in his ministry. The other candidate he had the privilege to pass on his apostolic succession was Mr. Eaton while he was in Tweed. He was serving Flinton, the nearest town to the north. Mr. Eaton went to India as an agriculturist teaching local people how to drill wells. A funny place to go when his wife was afraid of snakes. Chester was sure that he would make a great contribution wherever he found himself. Chester became a good friend with Ira Nigh who became a Licensed Lay Preacher in the United Church of Canada. A lifelong dream fulfilled when he received his certificate. Chester was present and participated in that ceremony.

The church was built after the fashion of a Presbyterian church. Two aisles divided the congregation into three sections. However the platform was too narrow to accommodate the massive furniture being used. It might have been moved from another building after the platform was built. The distance between the pulpit and the middle of three chairs was so narrow that there was no room to move but to stand at one place throughout the service. More serious than that, it forced Chester to drop his head in order to read from the pulpit Bible. This crunched his voice box and he was unable to speak loud enough to be heard. By rearranging the three chairs, it allowed him to stand back away from the pulpit and gave him room and his voice box to move normally. This solved his problem but it created another problem for the people. They could not understand why the smallest of the recent preachers had to move furnitures around. One day, he explained to his Official Board what prompted him to rearrange the furniture and he could hear a big sigh of relief now that the mystery had been solved.

Now that the running water issue and the flushing toilet were no longer issues in his life, he relaxed a bit and even thought of enjoying himself. He took up playing the Highland bagpipes again. There were a small group of bagpipe players in Ridgeway who just started a little band. He joined them as one of the players. They were all young people and they had a lot of fun together. They outfitted themselves with Highland kilts and practiced faithfully every Sunday afternoon. Unfortunate they lacked an instructor to lead them. Nevertheless they appeared in one of the smaller parades in the area. Word soon got around and they received some help from other bands in terms of instruction and equipment. They acquitted themselves creditably for being a small group with very little sponsorship from others. Unfortunately after only a short time, Chester left Ridgeway. They carried on without him. Later on, he was contacted by a young man who was interested in getting a set of pipes and to join the band. Chester sold him his pipes. Playing the pipes was among the last things Chester did during the four years he stayed in Ridgeway.

Another adventure was a second attempt to make himself a car length leather jacket. Chester had the good fortune of having a lady who worked as a dress designer in his congregation. She supported and encouraged him in the project. There was no such pattern available from Vogue or other catalogues. So he ordered an Eisenhower type jacket from Sears mail order. After he took the pattern off the jacket, he returned it for a refund. How naughty and clever of him at the same time. He went to the tannery and chose two pieces of glove leather and proceeded to cut out the pattern. Other necessary equipment included a chisel type sewing needle, some contact cement glue and then he proceeded to sew pieces together. He learned from his designer lady how to make an in seam pockets, how to measure for the inner linings out of silk and successfully finished the project. It was quite presentable. He made several copies afterward and gave three of them to his friends. They were all really impressed with what he managed to learn and accomplish. Chester was quite proud of himself.

Gerald Hesser was certainly one of his friends. He introduced him to play golf on the driving range. He married a local high school teacher who helped him develop his career. He rose from a field worker with the Union Gas to be the Region Vice President. He secured a contract with a glass manufacturer to sell them natural gas to heat the material so that it could be bent into automobile windshields. Just imagine the amount of natural gas necessary to soften the glass to the point that it could be bent into different shape. That was the kind of sale he generated at that level of corporate leadership. No small piece of change. With that kind of vision working for the church, Ridgeway grew and prospered while he headed the financial campaign to update the church's furnace and the pipe organ.

Bill Burger was a kind of intellect who was led astray by negativism and pessimism of the world. He was a mink farmer who obtained a license from the Department of Wildlife to confine wild animals in order to research the promulgation of minks. Meanwhile he slaughtered the animals at the fall and auctioned their fur in Montreal. That was his livelihood and income. He graduated in Agriculture from Quelph, Ontario and specialize in animal husbandry. His goal was to develop a kind of mink fur maximizing the blue component. He raised mink in the same fashions that poultry farmers cared for the animal. He invested heavily in a walk-in refrigerator to store his feed for mink, chiefly fish products brought in by 18 wheelers. He was in a very competitive market, but with his scientific approach to proper diet, he managed to be among the top producers of mink fur sought by furriers all over the world. His chief disappointment with organized religion was that spirituality was contaminated by human attempts to ritualize and organize it. In many ways, he was an idealist, while he had the proper vision of spirituality, he forgot the contribution by those who preserved it for others to scrutinize and to evaluate what was pure concept and what was human interpretations of it. It was a dichotomy that when humans attempted to give expression to a concept, they failed because of their linguistic limitations. The ocean was so great and humans were trying to empty it with their plastic buckets and shovels. Chester made no attempts to argue with him about religion but only to enjoy his friendship and appreciated who he was.  Sometimes Chester really wanted to know, whether he truly believes in what he said, or that was his way of avoiding his responsibility as a church member.  Only God would know.

~

# Chapter 18

## Superficiality, it will bite you

Chester always believed that respect was won from others. He always dressed himself appropriately. He behaved fittingly and never abused the social norm. There were those who conspired to take away his joy by taking advantage of his good nature and casted snide remarks that were hard to ignore. He had a fairly high tolerance of abuse from others because he belonged to a minority group. One such example was what happened while he was in Ridgeway.

Chester kept a faithful routine in his weekly schedule to include his hospital calls. He always dressed conservatively and appeared professional. On his return trip home, he made it his habit to stop at a grill and bar and get a cup of coffee. Usually the grill was filled with customers. On several occasions, the waitress who served him saw fit to practice what she thought was Chinese on Chester. It was a source of embarrassment and Chester chooses to ignore her and just smiled in return. This went on for several weeks. One Monday afternoon, Chester decided to confront her with her abuse. As soon as he entered the door, Rosie greeted Chester with the same gibberish across the length of the counter. Chester answered her with a voice loud enough to be heard by everyone,

"Lady, did you know what you just said to me? You said, 'I like to go to bed with you tonight.'"

There was a long moment of silence, everything stopped and you could hear a pin drop on the floor. Everyone was waiting for an appropriate response from the waitress. Her face instantly turned red as a beet and she just withdrew to the kitchen and was never seen again.

Apparently she had a boyfriend who just returned from a tour in South east Asia, and she was anxious to learn from him to say something in Chinese. Unbeknown to her, she was taught something that was totally self serving to his own need.

Chester had great respect for a culture that had a history of over four thousand years. The language was exquisite. Too many trifled with such treasure thinking that having learn only two phrases they had mastered enough to represent him/herself as competent in conversation. Such brashness was inexcusable and an insult to a whole nation.

What was the moral of this story. "Choose your friends carefully. Develop respect for others, especially those from another culture. Strive for excellence in whatever you are doing."

~

# Chapter 19

## Millville

Chester came to United States with a student visa which required renewal every year. Since he was a student pastor with the United Methodist Church, he qualified as a religious worker. By switching over to the new status, he had permanent residence and a green card. Eventually he applied and received his American citizenship but not until after Nixon left the White House.

Chester made overtures to Colgate Rochester Divinity School about their curriculum and his enrollment in their Master of Theology program while he was in Ridgeway Canada. Concurrently he wrote to the District Superintendent of the Methodist church about possible employment with them. After receiving a reply from him, they arranged to meet in Medina.

"You must be Mr. Louie," a middle age man dressed in a conservative dark blue suit and red tie greeted Chester, his wife and two young children.

"You must be Mr. Doyle of the Methodist Church." They shook hands heartily and found themselves seated in the restaurant.

"Did you have any trouble finding this place?" Mr. Doyle asked.

"Your instruction was very precise and we had no trouble following the route."

"I understand that you intend to enroll in Colgate Rochester Divinity School in the M.Th. Program?"

"I have talked with Dr. Wynn and he said that everything was in order."

"It is a good school. As a matter of fact, I graduated from the school many years ago. You are very fortunate to have Dr. Wynn on your team, he will be a good friend to have. He certainly is a good professor, a good scholar who published many books in the field of Christian Education."

"We had a very good interview."

"I understand that you are interested in working for the Methodist Church as a student pastor while you are attending school. How long have you been working for the United Church of Canada?"

"I was ordained in 1952. I served four pastorates with them, two in Saskatchewan and two in Ontario. My last congregation was in Ridgeway, Ontario."

"I know Ridgeway and Crystal Beach, Ontario very well. We spent a summer vacation there with the kids when they were small. They enjoyed the amusement park very much."

As they enjoyed the food under the candlelight from the chandelier, they continued with the conversation.

"I know that the Methodist Church in Canada merged with the Presbyterians in 1925 to form the United Church of Canada. There is so much in common between us that it is hard to tell the difference in our worship and church government. So I expect that you will be able to fit in the Methodist Church without any difficulty. We will be glad to have you help us in filling some of the vacant spots in the Western New York Conference and the Rochester District. We have two possible situations that will fill your needs. We can arrange to have you come over another time and discuss the situation in more detail. One congregation is engaged in the finishing stage of refurbishing the Christian Education wing of the church. Have you any experience in any building project with the church?"

"Yes, we just concluded a financial campaign to upgrade our pipe organ and the heating system. Everyone was happy and considered it a good experience of working together as a congregation in addition to working in a Fowl Supper every year."

"Now may I suggest that we meet again a week from today and we will go to the two places I have in mind and look over the situation. Would that suit you?"

"Sounds wonderful to me. I am looking forward to working with the Methodist Church. It would be a new experience for us to be working in the United States."

Millville was an intersection between two highways in the New York state. It was just that. It was a bedroom town with residents working in Batavia, Buffalo and Rochester. The church was just finishing up refurbishing the Christian Education wing from an old barn. The parsonage was small but adequate. When they heard that Chester was coming with two small children, they finished the upstairs of the parsonage and turned it into a small bedroom.

Millville had only one service in the morning and a Sunday school beforehand. It had a congregation between 50 to 75 in Sunday worship. The duties were very light during the week which allowed the pastor to engage in studies in Rochester. Everyone was very friendly and faithful in attendance. Members of the congregation were middle class, with a good number of school teachers, attorneys, long distance truck drivers and retirees. There was one general store for emergencies. The nearest center was Medina, where shopping was done and where the children were bused to school. Altogether it was a quiet place for a student to concentrate on his studies. Chester was so overjoyed. He nearly forgot to mention, it has running water and flush toilet.

When Chester interviewed with the Director of Study, Dr. J.C.Wynn about his Master of Theology Program, it was suggested that if he spent two years with them, he would have earned his M.Th. and also the Master of Divinity degree since he had already done the equivalent work in Canada.

It was one thing to enroll in the school, it was another thing to be acclimated to the accent of the American tongue. It took him at least three months to be at home with their speaking in lectures. It required Chester to tape record the psychology lectures and play it back three times in order to understand what Dr. Ashbrook was saying.

After the congregation finished the building project, he was given a study where he spent most of his time. Fortunately the study was separated from the house by a sixty foot driveway, so it was easy to slip to the parsonage to get a cup of tea and stretch his legs regularly. The Department of Pastoral Theology at the school, was within the Division of Christian Education. Courses dealing with human development and relationship were limited but he took all that were available. He also took classes from St. Bernard's Seminary, a Roman Catholic school affiliated with Colgate Rochester. Chester enrolled in one class called "Social Work for Priests." Essentially it was a review of social services and benefits available to help with children and family receiving government aids. He was looking for learning more on human interaction dynamics within a family. However he became familiar with their Celebration of the Eucharist and their lunch menu twice a week. During his second year, he interned with the Child Guidance Clinic, a part of the outpatient service of the residential home for children in Scottsville. There he was introduced to techniques of interviewing, diagnosing the problem and the approaches to treatment. His supervisors were a Clinical Social Worker and a Psychologist. It was a good learning experience which solidified further his desire to pursue marriage counseling as his career.

Graduation took place in the auditorium with all the pageantry available. The faculty with their colorful hoods and gowns followed the graduates as the pipe organ played the traditional processional music. The convocation address was given by one of their own staff, Harvey Cox, who wrote the book, "God is Dead." He left shortly to go to teach at the Harvard Divinity School. Chester was personally greeted by Dr. Wynn afterward, to celebrated the long journey started two years before. It was a happy occasion with friends from Millville as well as from Canada. It was a special moment to see Pa and Ma Elliott present. They travelled all the way from Tweed Ontario to witness this happy event.

With such brief exposure to Social Work, he spent sixteen months with the Rochester Council of Church Counseling Center. This brief period convinced him that he was not ready to solo as a counselor. What the small amount of pastoral care he learned, it was obviously borrowed from the other academic curriculum. At this time, he also began his individual therapy with a psychologist for three years on a weekly basis. That fulfilled requirements for New York state license as a practitioner in counseling. Through the experience of undergoing private counseling, Chester was convinced of the need to engage in graduate study for a Master of Social Work at Syracuse University.

Shortly after his graduation with his Master of Theology degree, his first wife died. Chester had the good fortune to meet a lady in his congregation in Livonia who became his present spouse. Allene is a musician, a scholar, a professional and a good mother. She encouraged and supported Chester to go to Syracuse for his M.S.W. while he continued to work as a student pastor and she as a supervisor for the Rochester Visiting Nurse Service. He really immersed himself in Social Work study with emphasis in group work. There was no text book available to deal with the dynamics between persons at the time. Without exaggeration, materials for the lecture were printed from mimeograph machine just before class. The ink was still wet if they touched them accidentally. He interned with the Jewish Family Service for the first year and the Rochester School Board for the second year. He felt more comfortable about the practice of counseling in the real world.

Courtship and honeymoon were short but exciting. They toured the eastern coast and finally ended up at Bath, Maine, where they witnessed the construction of a ferrous cement ship while in drydock. At the same evening, the local church sponsored an organ recital by one of the summer cottage guest from Ohio. From there they went to Bar Harbor, Maine and camped overnight in their RV above the clouds on Cadillac Mountain overlooking the ferry, like a little sailboat in the bathtub.

Chester asked himself "What is a man going to do with three master degrees without a Ph.D.?" They discussed the advantage of earning an academic doctorate or a doctorate within the theological curriculum from Emory University. After much debate they decided that more opportunities were available with an academic doctorate from Syracuse University. This would open fields of teaching, or clinical work or private practice. After passing all the hoops of the doctoral program involved in classes and dissertation, he finally received his degree in the Carrier Dome on Syracuse campus with 46,000 applauding in the audience. What a sweet victory it was to redeem himself from the Grade 12, I.Q. Score of 86! That was one of his proudest moments of his life with due credit and support given by his wife, Allene.

If Chester had a nickel each time he was asked, "Where were you born?" or "Where do you come from?" he would have enough money to buy B.C. Electric and owning Wegman or Safeway grocery chain stores would only be pocket change. For thirty two years he spent in Canada, he was constantly bombarded with these questions. Is the Pope Catholic? Isn't it obvious with slant eyes and the sallow complexion, did you need to ask? In his attempt to account for such rhetoric, he reasoned that it was the people's attempt to satisfy their curiosity for the mongrel brand of English that came from his mouth. In Vancouver, the only criterion of Anglo Saxon English was the Irish and Scottish brogue. Later on, especially in Saskatchewan, the question switched to "What is your nationality?" By that time, he took an offensive posture in his answer and began to respond by saying, "My mother was born in the kibbutz in Israel and my father came from Serbia, Russia. So I really don't know what that makes my nationality." Usually they changed the subject or they walked away. Either way they got the message.

Since he came to USA, he was asked less frequently the question "Where did you come from?" Partly because, there was a multi cultural accent among themselves, from the Blacks, Italian, Jewish, Russian German and the rest of the world, and partly because they couldn't understand each other. Even the northern folk could not understand the southern black. "Dark color shoes" sounded like "Dog color shoes." Diversity is to be celebrated in the "melting pot", which is America.

~

# Chapter 20

## Livonia by the Lake

Livonia, a bedroom community serving Rochester was located on the Conesius Lake. It had one main street running up the hill and five avenues running at right angle to it. The lake was large enough to have east lake road and west lake road around it. Permanent residences lined the beach front, punctuated with summer cottages. There was always activities on the lake, sailing boats with brightly decorated canvass fluttering in the breeze during summer and plastic wind breakers to shelter ice fishermen when the lake was frozen over.

The town was built on a giant slope, steep enough to challenge any skateboard artist to navigate down hill from Summer Street to the other edge of town. There was the usual post office on main street, a hardware and a grocery shop on main street as well as a library. The main shopping was done in Geneva only ten miles away. Any serious shopping was done in Rochester a city forty minutes on a divided highway.

For Chester, the first question was to ask "Has the town a water and sewage system?" After that, "Where is the school for the children?" The town had a good water and sewage systems. The elementary and the high school were located in town, while the buses transported children from twenty five mile radius.

There were two Protestant congregations in Livonia , which eventually merged together and built a new building on Summer Street. The Methodist church was a wooden frame structure with a full basement where the Sunday Sunday was held. The upper and lower levels were connected with a narrow staircase which allowed only for one way traffic. To show how impressionable children were, adults must be careful on what they teach them. It was somewhat awesome and humbling to overhear what one six year old boy said as he held back the traffic to let Chester descend downstairs. "Wait up for a minute, here comes God, let him come down first." It must have been quite a frightening sight for him to see a silhouette at the head of the stair, trying to come down to his level.

Chester and his family arrived at Livonia in July. Unfortunately in
September, his wife took sick and was taken to Roswell Hospital in Buffalo NY because the brain tumor had come back. Only palliative care was given and she lapsed into a coma. Eventually she passed away without wakening up from the comma. It was a tragic time for the children to lose their mother and for Chester to lose his spouse. A memorial service was held and her ashes were buried in the Livonia cemetery.

At that time, the shoulder strap purse became popular. Denise wanted one for Christmas. Chester tried his best to find one for her. All he saw in Livonia stores were purses with two straps. He knew that would not foot the bill. Somehow Chester knew that he could be a father to Denise but never a mother, who would go shopping until a single strap purse was found. Chester resolved that for the sake of the children, he must find his help mate. He thoroughly believed that providence interceded and provided the right person. He found her among the ladies in his congregation, she sat in the left section and the third row from the front. Her brother sang in the choir, therefore it was easy to ask him for an introduction. After a short dating period, they were married. That was forty three years ago. She was a musician, played the accordion, violin and the cello and sang in the high school choir who took the New York State championship. She passed the ten point screening Chester had in mind for his spouse. But she later told him that he passed the thirteen point screening test for her life partner. She earned her master's degree in nursing from Buffalo University. So she was an intellectual as well. On their honeymoon, they motored cross country to the east coast and visited Maine. They tracked down the dry dock where a "ferrous cement fishing boat" was made as well as camping on top of Cadillac Mountain in the Acadia National Park among the clouds looking down at the water below as the ferry Blue Nose was leaving for Halifax Nova Scotia.

"We have heard of the ferrous cement ship and we have come to see it for ourselves. Is this the right place?"

"Yes, you have come to the right place. My name is Harvey, what is yours?"

"I am Chester, and she is my wife, Allene."

"Very please to meet you both. Where is home for you?"

"We came from Rochester, New York."

"How did you come to hear about us?"

"I read it in a magazine many months ago. But this is the first chance we have to come across country to the east coast."

"I am the superintendent for the crew who builds the ship. Follow me and I will be glad to show you around and answer any question you may have."

"The first question is about the weight. Cement is always connected with weight. How can you float the block of cement?"

"A solid block of cement will sink, but a hollow bowl made of cement will float nicely."

"Ships are made from wood. Isn't cement heavier than wood?"

"They are about the same. We use two inch steel pipe and bend them into the shape we want. Instead of tying them by nails or rivets, we weld them together. Then we cover them with seven layers of screens used in making fences. We then draw the seven layers of screen tightly together with smaller wires. By the time we finish, the wall are very much solid as one piece. Then we press cement into the seven layers of chicken screens until the wall is three inches thick. Of course we take time to cure them properly. The actual process is proprietary and a trade secret.."

"I still think that the cement is heavier than wood."

"You have to remember that when we use wood to cover the ribs, we use at least three inch thick planks of white oak. Have you ever try to muscle a plank of white oak? It is heavy, and many workers' backs were injured. While cement covered wall for the hull of a ship may sound heavy, they weigh about the same."

"When it comes to repair, can you patch a hole in the cement?"

"We do it the same way we would repair any wood surface. First we clean out the edges and then apply the same material to fill the hole."

"Is this new technology you develop?"

"Not by any means. The Italians built a ferrous cement ship many years ago and it was very successful."

"Why now?"

"We are running out of white oak in the country. It is very scarce and very hard to find. I suppose we can build the ship with steel, but it is so romantic to revive an ancient method to do things. The good thing is that it works......Follow me and we can see one in the process of being built. It is commision by XYZ. Instead of building a yacht, he wanted to do something new. After the hull is finished, we will install the engine and the interior."

"It certainly is very impressive. This must be sixty five feet long, would you say?"

"It is going to be seventy five feet long and it will have three decks. It is built to travel in open water. She is a beauty. After it's finish with a couple coat of paint, I dare say you could not tell the difference unless you were told that it was made of cement. Just think what a conversation starter in any port."

"Have you built one before?"

"I personally oversaw the construction of at least four others. They all turn out just perfect and the owners said they won't have it any other way."

"We are very pleased to have seen this today and thanks for all the education you've given us. It certainly is interesting to hear about the ferrous cement ship. Is this the only shipyard who builds ferrous cement ships?"

"I can't say for sure. There might be others, but I haven't heard of them. If there were others, I would sure like to contact them and talk shop with them."

"We must go and thank you again for your guided tour. Good luck."

"Good bye for now.  Where are you heading to, you said you came from Rochester NY?"

"We are thinking of going to Bar Harbor.  Is it very far from here?"

"It's not too far.  If you are free tonight, there is an organ recital in our church.  He has a cottage in our area, he always agreed to play the organ once a year, so we can raise money to keep our church and the pipe organ in good shape.  It is at 8 o'clock at the church.  I hope you can take advantage of it, if you like that kind of music."

"Indeed we will be there.  We won't miss it for all the tea in China."

~

# Chapter 21

## Bridge to the end

The church to which Chester was assigned in Rochester was located within the inner city. When women drove up Joseph Avenue, they always locked the door from the inside. That was the atmosphere of violence in that area. The children walked six blocks to Franklin High School. It was a dicey adventure everyday for them. Fortunately during the two years there, there was no incidence.

The church was located at the corner of Joseph Avenue and Farbridge. There was an addition to the church which they used as the Christian Education wing. On top of this section was the apartment for the pastor and his family. There were three bedrooms, a sitting room, dining room and a kitchen at the back. In the closet of one of the bedroom was the end of 32 foot pipe of the pipe organ. On Sunday morning when the organist turned up promptly at 8 o'clock to warm up the instrument, it provided the alarm for the pastor to get up and get ready for the day's routine. It would be most aggravating, to be awakened by the base notes of the music, were it not for his love of the instrument.

The study on the second floor, had an outside window that led to a ledge. It was a favorite place where all the pigeons huddled to keep warm. They greeted each other with their typical cooing sound continuously. This distraction was most annoying when Chester wanted to concentrate on his study. There was no way to discourage the pigeons from their perch on the ledge, Chester tried to put a rubber snake with no effect. He tried to put molasses on the ledge hoping that the animal would find their feet sticking to the ledge, but to no avail. Unfortunately, the neighbor across the street counteract any of Chester's effort to rid the animal by throwing bread crumbs inside the yard immediately under the ledge every morning. Being a man of good will, Chester did not want to offend anyone, he just ignored his daily practice of littering the church yard.

Chester and his wife focused on the reason why they lived in this situation. It was to have lodging for the family while Chester went to study at Syracuse for his graduate degree in Social Work. He spent two days attending lectures and two day interning at Clifford Technical school and later at the Jewish Family service for experience. This continued for two years after which the church was closed and the building was sold to an Hispanic congregation.

Reflecting back on the nature of the graduate school curriculum for MSW, there were outstanding incidences which came to mind. One of the memorable class taught in communication was in the form of a demonstration to show how essential it was to get feedback in order to achieve accurate communication. A student was to sit in front with his back to the class. The task was to get the class to reproduce a drawing or image given to him by the instructor.

"Without using your hands, or posturing of your body or any other aids such as drawing on the chalkboard, describe to the class this drawing." The class is to reproduce the drawing from his instruction.

The drawing has two main components. There is a right angle triangle with the right angle pointed toward the lower right hand corner of the page. The hypotenuse, faces the upper left corner of the page. Find the midpoint of the hypotenuse and call that point 'X'. Draw any circle with the common point of contact at point X. The general shape of the drawing is to show a ball rolling down an incline plane.

It was surprising how a simple drawing could create so much confusion among the class. It presumed a little knowledge of geometry and be able to identify parts of the triangle. At least ten students tried to describe the drawing without success. If the class had a chance to ask question concerning the particular terms of the triangle or if there was any doubt, all the rest is quite straight forward. It was a good exercise to spotlight the importance of feedback in any conversation.

The second incidence during the program was an exercise involving the class in group dynamics.

One day, the instructor appeared in class dressed in overalls which was out of character for him. He made only one announcement before he sat down among the chairs in the room. "For the next forty minutes, here are the rules. (1) No one can leave the room. (2) There will be no drink or food allowed." With that he sat down in one of the chairs among the students.

For the first three minutes, there were perfect silence. Everyone was waiting for something to happen. Then one student spoke and asked what are they supposed to do. There were several answers from fellow students, some showed disappointment for the lack of structure, one blamed the instructor for lack of preparation. One complained that this was an absolute waste of his time and there were other more pressing things to do. After all the frustrations were vented, one student insisted that the instructor took charge. The instructor acted as if he did not hear what was said and sat emotionless. Gradually the class attempted to draw up an agenda and offered suggestion as to what they could do for the remaining period of time. One suggested that they could play a game of twenty questions. One said that they could play "Simon Says." Another like to idea of just sitting quiet for the remaining time. None of them were taken up with any support. There was silence again. When the forty minutes were up, the instructor took his place in the front of the class and said, "You have just demonstrated to yourselves how a group may act on its own without structure. The group has a character of its own. It has personality, it has power. It can show murderous rage, it can show control of it's own members. It can support as well as destroy. It does not like a vacuum, it looks for leadership. A crowd feels more comfortable to follow whoever can command the situation. There is implicit leadership for the group, and there is conferred leadership. There is power in a group. The lesson for us today is to be aware that these things are taking place, and you as leader in any group need to know and learn how to manage it. The class is now over. Have a good day."

Thinking back about the graduate work in MSW, Chester's impression centered around two things. During each semester, each student was required to write at least twenty term papers, if not thirty. That was a lot of writing. In fact the final grade for each course was based on the marks received on the term paper. The second thing that remain in his mind was that the program leant toward the idea of individual supervised independent study. If a student was under a proper mentor, he could do all the"Literature Review' a component of the doctoral dissertation and presented them as term papers. Just imagine the amount of time one could save if he were so advised. Nevertheless, the master level of study was very good preparation to writing and reporting the research to come. Very valuable principles were learned to proper interviewing techniques, and the basic knowledge of human development, which were essential to any helping process.

Meanwhile Chester graduated with his MSW and felt ready to set up private practice in counseling. He was already accepted into the doctoral program at Syracuse. They bought a house close to the Strong Hospital and started with four patients. Coincident to his master's work, he also started having therapy with E Donald Smith a psychologist as requirement for a license as a private practitioner in counseling in New York State. Life was busy between study, private practice, his own therapy and work as a social worker for a nursing home. He was nearly side tracked when the largest United Church in Vancouver invited him to set up a counseling center at the church. Considering everything that was going on, he declined and worked toward the completion of study with Syracuse University. The dissertation stage was a hurdle. After a false start, he finally completed the work and passed his oral defense. The data was drawn from a National Survey conducted by Dean of the Social Worker School, who created an interviewed of a random sample of all Americans over 65 age of age. The first interview took two and a half hours detailing the effect of community services availability to their health. Nine months later, a random sample was re interviewed for a longitudinal study. The data base was so massive, it took two graduate assistants four years to punch the IBM cards. At least four doctoral studies drew on this data base. It was manipulated by computer without human interference. Soon after his graduation with his Ph.D. he was invited to go to Boston to head up the Mental Health Department of a community health center.

~

# Chapter 22

## Boston

After Chester received his doctorate from Syracuse University, an unexpected new horizon was opened to him. He had a job offer from Boston, Massachusett, who was looking for a Director of Mental Health in a community health center. It was attractive in many ways because of the location as well as a new opportunity in terms of career development.

Who has not heard of Boston? Every child in school is familiar with the Pilgrims landing in Plymouth. It is the cradle of the American colony. The story of Paul Revere signaling the message "the British are coming" become the epitome of heroism. Every school pageant around Thanksgiving time includes a scene of the Pilgrims, with Indians and turkeys, along with bright orange pumpkins.

Not only is Boston known for its historical pre-eminence, it is considered to be the playground of the rich and famous. Anyone and everyone who aspired to be a celebrity have their pictures taken in Martha's Vineyard. Not only is Boston noted as the stomping places of the Kennedys, it is the premier sites of higher learning. The names of Harvard and M.I.T are respected all over the world. We are talking about the creme de la creme. A Harvard M.B.A. from their School of Business will get you through the door of any corporation in the world. The city is not lacking in its cultural luster. The Boston Symphony and the Boston Pop are household names among the patrons of the arts.

The city of Boston ranks among the most popular choice of world travellers as representing the quintessence of Americanism. New York City has its Fifth Avenue, the Macy Store, and the Laguardia Airport, as well as the Central Park, but Boston has its Commonwealth Avenue, Logan International Airport and the Boston Commons. All these amenities leap to Chester's mind when he heard the mention of Boston over the phone. What an adventure lays in his future?

To Chester, Boston means a new career opportunity. He has a chance to advance his career. It being a cosmopolitan center, many new possibilities are available to him. With a license in Massachusete as a Clinical Social Worker, his skills and training will be recognized and rewarded. The cultural enriched environment and the "big pond" to develop his professional skills made it a win-win situation too tempting to refuse.

As soon as he received his license, he took advantage of the new found alternative to set up private practice in marriage counseling. Because he can claim dual competence in two fields, Theology and the "helping process" from Social Work, he received many referrals from clergies in Boston, who has neither the depth of counseling skill nor the time to devote to this part of their ministry. Soon he has a caseload of his choice in numbers. Many of his patients worked in big companies like Raytheon who have Blue Cross/Blue Shield health coverage. With his free time, he was able to test his skills in the industrial world. He found an opportunity to do research for a plastic injection company. They were looking for a researcher to work out a projected schedule of maintenance for their seventy plus molds to avoid unscheduled repair delaying their delivery deadline. He had no experience working with machines, but he knew statistics and how to do a stepwise regression analysis. Such analysis can be applied to any situation to find the most significant contributing factor to the dependent variable. He was given an air condition office and a twenty six thousand dollar computer to do the work. He was also given the same software as used by the aerospace engineers in Boeing Company. Essentially he was given the job of heading the computer division of the company. Along with doing the research, he was asked to organize and produce a catalog of their inventory. Also each month, he sent a featured item to advertise in a trade magazine involving photographic work.

Once a week, he volunteered his time to a singles group as program coordinator. During lunch time, he took a folding lawn chair to a cemetary, found a shady spot under a big oak tree and wrote the manuscript of his first book, "1000 Voices in the Thunder." He managed to squeeze in a two week vacation in Sweden. These activities took most of his energies, but he relished the challenge and enjoyed the peak of his productivity.

Meanwhile, his wife was being trained as an administrator within the VA Hospital system. Her first appointment was to Salisbury, North Carolina VA Medical Center. He closed out his private practice and they arrived at Salisbury on February 17, 1990. He remembers the day very well. Crocketsis were blooming beside the road, while Boston was still buried deep in snow.

~

# Chapter 23

## Reflection of all his activities

In view of all the different fields Chester worked in, one would justifiably asked, "What are your thoughts as to what is important in your life? What would you like to share with the younger generations as they start out in their journey?"

With due modesty, I must say that I tried many things and enjoyed life fully. Blessed with abundance in every area of life, I am grateful to have started from the ghettos, and have come a long way. I like to pass on some thoughts which I consider as important which had guided me in my journey, and hopefully they will be helpful to others. These come from my heart and I feel that it would be more direct if I step out from Chester's person and speak using the first person posture. I hope that this change will make my message more personal to my audience.

~

# Chapter 24

## Who has all the answers?

The therapist doesn't, if he thinks he has, he should keep it to himself. Why? Because that is not what the patient wants. S/he wants to be listened to, be understood, accepted and to be validated, and in that order. There are good reasons to follow these steps, and it will become plain later on. For too long, the patient has been ignored, his problem dismissed or minimized, but those are his basic needs in life. When these are not fulfilled, all sort of il-behaviors surface and they take as many faces as there are individuals.

What is the role of the therapist and who is a good therapist? He doesn't have to know all the answers to every question? There are too many questions in this world and only a superman has the capacity to remember the answers to them all. Beside no two situations are identical. Each situation is different, each patient perceives the same situation differently according to his past experience. How he reacts now might be different two months from now. So the solution must be the patient's decision and something that s/he is willing to live with for a long time.

There is a great saying we may not understand the depth of its meaning. "The only thing you can be sure of is yourself." Another way to saying the same thing is "The only thing you know for sure is how do you feel about it. And even that, unless it comes from the patient, what you hear might be mistaken. You cannot get out of your own skin." Everything you know about the world, depends on the way you perceive the information. Everything you know about the patient is told by him. Any feelings you have about the patient is initiated by your patient and by your interpretation of that information. The important truth about this statement is that the better you know about yourself, the better you know your tendency to interpret the information given to you. What flaws you have in relating to people will determine how accurately you are able to know the world that lies outside of you. That is the reason why a good clinician needs to undergo three hundred hours of therapy as part of the requirement for licensure. We will not digress beyond this point, but just to illustrate why it is so important to give credence to the statement here, here is a good example. It is deplorable for someone to say, "I know how you feel." A patient has every right to say in anger, "dog-gone it, but you don't know how I feel, how can you, you were never in my shoes, you never have to live with that man for fifteen years, you haven't heard the verbal abuse that came from his filthy mouth, you never had to put up with his temper when he is drunk. How can you begin to know how I feel?" Well said, all that is true, absolutely true."

A good therapist will learn to disarm such ferocious assault by saying, "I was never in your shoes, I do not live with that man and only you will know the frustration and anger he evokes. But help me to understand the situation in your house for the last fifteen years, what is it like when he is drunk or angry? What sort of things he threw at you in fits of anger? I like to know what fear you have when he is in one of his fits." That is the reason why psychologist and clinician had to invent a new word "empathy." Sympathy means to be one with the patient, to be completely absorbed in her anger, fear and frustration, to the point where the therapist abandoned his own selfhood. That is counterproductive. More importantly, that is too much to carry on your shoulder when you meet with two or four such patients in a day. They can sap all the joy out of your life, and you have no more to give to your next patient. To empathize with your patient means to stand beside him/her, conveying the feeling that you heard what she said and understood the reason why she felt that way. You acknowledge she has the right to feel how she felt and there is no judgment on your part. The goal is to impart acceptance. To do that successfully, it means not to let your own problems get in the way. To keep an open mind and be ready to hear what the patient tells you. A famous illustration of acceptance is when the patient is ready to tell you he has committed murder, your reply is "How many?" That sounds so trite. But it is true, to concentrate on his needs without your own baggage of unresolved fear and anger to get in the way. An exaggerate example of poor counselling is for the therapist to unload his hard day schedule on the patient. Such was the case when a caregiver sought help to deal with his depression. "My son, you think you had a hard day, let me share with you the trouble that your neighbor had with his dog, who was absolutely abominable. Blah, blah....." When he finished, the caregiver was made to feel ashame to have taken his time with his little bit of weakness. The counselor might just as well have said, "Suck it up, be thankful that you are still alive. You could have been in the insane asylum."

What are the skills of a therapist and who could be a therapist?

The internship program is an integral component of a graduate school program in Social Work. While the classroom teaches the theoretical component of Social Work, the practical skill of a social worker is learned from the supervision of a mentor through weekly discussion on a "virtual" interaction between the student and the patient. There is no way to hide from the realism of an actual interview room. The role play situation in a classroom offers a moment, if only two seconds, to frame a proper response to a hypothetical situation. The student must leaned to think on his feet, and there is no better place than to be in the front line by doing it. Among the first thing he learns is to ask open questions, such as "Can you explain what you mean when you....,"or "Can you elaborate on this point that you just made?" Never frame a question that can be answered with a yes or no. Learn to use words like "Can you help me to understand what....., when....., how..... and why....." Don't let the patient off too easily, make him work in the therapy session. There is a huge amount of material given in each interview session. One must learn to organize them by having a theoretical framework to hang them in their proper place. That is where theory comes in. The field of Social Work is interdisciplinary knowledge-based on studies, accumulated from the research done in the past. Though they are only theory, waiting to be proven wrong, until it is done, it serves well to explain much of what they encounter with the patient. That is why courses are often called theory and practice. The two aspects go hand in hand and each support the other. Among the best ways to explain behavior is that proposed by Sigmund Freud. His terminologies of behaviors have been incorporated into everyday English vocabulary. Other theories of behavior were proposed by Erikson, Piaget and Maslow, just to name a few. Generally it states that the fundamental physical needs must be met before the next higher social and spiritual needs can be developed. If the rudimentary building blocks necessary for mental health are not met, one becomes fixated at that level. One cannot grow to the next step of development. These theories are sufficient to explain many causes of behavior, they are still theories, waiting to be disproved.

Chester started out thinking that specific behavior requires specific treatment. As in Medicine, a tonsillitis require surgery to remove the culprit, an allergy reaction necessitates desensitization to the allergen. Not so in Mental Health. The theory of human behavior believes that when basic needs like emotional stability and self acceptance are not met, ill-behavior will surface. The form and shape will differ in as many form as there are individuals. To illustrate: when an individual is unfulfilled and prevented from reaching his/her fullest potential, his behavior will show in a number of symptoms. It can take the form of bed wetting to arson, from shingles to psoriasis and skin rashes. In the case of someone who could not find employment in the field he was trained and forced to work at a menial job below his potential, he turned to anger toward members of his family, toward his church and toward all his friends. Through proper exploration of his past background and by creative means of introducing him to retraining, he was able to find fulfillment in life and recapture his dignity and self worth. He was able to let go his negativism toward the world and became a contributing member of the community, a loving spouse, good member of his church and a joy to his friends. Although it took many years of work to bring him to this goal, it requires patience and commitment on both sides but it is possible.

The most rewarding case was to practice the Conjoint family therapy model.

While the presenting patient was a 12 year old child with bed wetting problem, the whole family with the grandmother, both parents and two other siblings were asked to come and interact with each other in the same room for thirty minutes. It presented a unique demonstration of the dynamics which existed in the family that caused the problem. The patient was the middle child, the older brother was forteen years old, while the youngest member of the family was six years old. The dynamics between the six individuals were acted out vividly and no amount of writing and description would do justice to fully describe what was going on. The three boys each was vying for mothers attention, the father sat passively throughout the session without saying a word, the mother had her hands full caring for the six year old still in diaper, while the grandmother was completely engross in her knitting. The boys were acting out and bullying each other, expecting the mother to be the umpire and keep the peace in the family. She was getting no help from her husband and out of absolute frustration, began to sob quietly. What a pathetic picture to witness. Upon separating the members of the group, each individual was interviewed individually. The picture became clear that the father gave up in frustration after five years of attempts to give some leadership in maintaining some discipline. The grandmother admitted her distancing attitude because her daughter was born out of wedlock. She still felt the guilt of her mistake of sex before marriage and was determined not to interfere with the upbringing of the grandchildren fearing that the mother will make another mistake.  Meanwhile the mother struggled by herself to do the best she could.  Each child had different needs.  The eldest of the three boys felt that someone should be the head of the house .  When he saw his father was ineffective, he lost all respect for his father.  He was only trying to help his mother to maintain some control on his unruly brothers.  The patient saw that his youngest brother was getting more than his share of attention and became jealous of him.  Though he sought to get close to his grandmother for support, he was rejected by referring him back to his father, who again rejected him and referred him to his mother.  The patient was confused as to who is the real authority in the family.  With this instability in his life, and the precipitating reminder that his mother's favorite was centered in his younger brother, he was afraid that he might lost his place in the family.  Through systematic clarification for each person in the family, each one was helped to see what went awry and what needed to be corrected before normalcy can be restored.  There were really thirty sets of dynamics present and accounted for as each one interact with the other five persons in the family.

Another case came to mind which could have easily side-track many into a goose chase.  It concerned a woman who found herself absolutely frightened and panic stricken while driving her car when she was forced to wait at a stop light but sandwiched between two cars.  She would be more than willing to abandon her car, left it where it was and walked home by herself.  We tried desensitization method to no avail, nor hypnosis.  Finally Chester found that she witnessed the death of her brother who was impaled by a metal spike of the fence as he slid down the front step of their house.  After this exploration of that incidence and how she felt she was responsible, she was able drive normally in traffic.  Strange but true.

At the same time, one must learn to accept his limitation and resources to affect change.  A referral was made to Chester from one of the churches.  The presenting problem was that this woman physically kicked her daughter in the rear in the cloakroom of the church when she was acting out.  After interviewing with the daughter, she was asked to wait in their car while her mother was seen in private.  The daughter must have grown bored waiting, she proceeded to set fire among the brushes in the yard.  Before the fire was discovered, Chester heard from the mother that they were brought up on the farm and resented being uprooted to live in a city without her support system.  Further interviews reveal the information that the absent father drove a long distance truck route across the continent.  They just barely made ends meet.  The 13 year old daughter was not doing well in school and was threatened to be expelled by the school authority more than two occasions.  Chester realized there were many facets to the situation.  Attention must be given to help the daughter, to deal with her level of frustration and control of her anger, the mother required long term therapy to help her with her social skill, resolution to her relationship with her spouse, and her basic unhappiness in her social isolation.  But the most critical issue was her unwillingness to commit to long term therapy for both the daughter and herself.  Chester realize his limited resource of time and scheduling and he was forced to make a referral to the psychiatrist.  Unfortunately she did not follow through.  One thing caregivers must learn to accept , that you cannot overextend yourself and must learn your limitation and keep your own sanity.

A good therapist helps the patient to identify the root of the problem, the cause of the problem, to explore alternative solution to his problem, to implement the decision he decides to follow.

~

# Chapter 25

## How to be your best self.

Specialists like Sidney M Jourard, who study the contributing factors to any long lasting meaningful relationship name at least three important components; they are authenticity, transparency and vulnerability. There is such a thing as instant physical attraction, some call this kind of feeling, lusts or falling in love. Physical attributes change through time, glamors depends much on fashion. They come and go. But here we are focusing on the other kind of love, the sustaining, committed kind, the kind that abides through all changes in a lifetime.

Authenticity starts with self knowledge, knowing who s/he is, and dares to be himself or herself. From the healthy development of childhood, a certain amount of self esteem is attained, a strong ego enables the individual to present himself to others without the need to wear a mask or to hide behind something or someone. There is a popular saying nowaday, "What you see is what you get," typifies this attitude. This self assured attitude should be tempered with a good dose of humility. This ability to be yourself come also from maturity after a period of self assessment of strength and weakness. It has the self assurance that what he is, is positive and is worthy of respect from others. It has no fear of rejection by others, knowing that he has a rightful place in society. He has no need to pretend to be someone he is not. He stands on his own.

Transparency is built on authenticity. Because he knows who he is, he allows others to see who he is. This is necessary to develop closeness and intimacy with others. Many are forever hiding behind something or someone because he is afraid that others will find weakness in his characters.

Transparency enable others to know you and relate to you. No one wants to waste time talking to a ghost. Communication involves a great deal of investment of time and energy. Transparency is the willingness to be seen. It precede knowing others. A good practice in relationship when seeking information from others, is to start with revealing something of yourself. For example, "My name is Chester, what is yours? "Have you ever met someone who are very secretive about his coming and going? Chester once talked to someone who works for the FBI as an undercover agent to infiltrate an organization. Of course, he doesn't want others to know his true identity. He is an exception to the general rule. Many people believe that hidden knowledge is power. It does not work in relationship. No one except children wants to invest in make-belief.

Vulnerability is the willingness to risk rejection. Everyone hates rejection, But it is countered with self esteem. Rejection is a dangerous thing to deal with, it gives rise to self doubt and destroys self esteem. In spite of the possible cost, we continue to exercise it because it inspires vulnerability in others. As one shares with others, closeness develops, barriers come down, and it eventuated in intimacy.

In order to have all these three components operating, communication must be kept open and allow to flow freely. Therefore our conversation is purposeful. That does not mean to say that we should be serious all the time but we should remember what is the overall agenda. The goal is to develop closeness, to establish closeness at a higher level. When two spirits resonate in the same frequency, true intimacy is formed. When they arrive at this level, they are ready to make this intimacy long lasting and ready for all the responsibilities attach to total abandonment to each other.

These qualities aforementioned are the building blocks of every good friendship. With members of the opposite sex, one may choose to deepen the friendship to the next level of interaction commonly called love. Genuine friendship is developed over time. When one is serious during this period, it has specific tasks to accomplish. It is the time to explore more thoroughly the personality of the other person. While one is having fun together, it is also a time to notice the likes and dislikes of the other person. Conversation takes on more intensity to find out what are the goals and the dreams s/he has. What kind of ambitions lodges in his mind, as well as testing his potential and ability. One seeks to know, how committed s/he is to achieving his dreams. At this time, one is trying to determine how compatible s/he is to your own values and whether the two of you have enough in common so that the future can be spent in building the same dreams together or not. Not to look for a duplicate of yourself, but there should be enough commonality so that you can be partners in life's journey together.

Not only do you seek to know the other person more deeply, one wants to get to know his family, for one's' value system originates from the family in which he grows up. The social environment determines the person's expectation in life. The interaction between the parents give valuable clues to what can be expected in the future. If there is calm and security in the home , very likely the other person seeks to reproduce the same atmosphere in her own home. If you notice a lack of organization or lack of problem solving skill, very likely you will see in him the same pattern of "flying by the seat of your pants." Habits of good housekeeping are taught by osmosis, never by words. Our parents provide the norms on what is acceptable and what is not in morality. While we can choose our friends but not our relatives, we can probably predict what can be expected in the future. Seeds are never far away from the tree above. It is time to determine if there is enough commonality between you, and enough complementarity to add variety and excitement in your future. There is a seriousness to this period, very specific tasks to accomplish to bring friendship to the next level of relationship.

When all the comparison among the candidates are evaluated, one makes the choice as to whom you are best suited to partner with in view of the responsibilities of marriage. I am impressed with the careful and elaborate preparations made before the wedding. I only wish the brides and grooms take equal time to ponder on the vows and covenants they are going to take on. While respect, trust and commitment are tested during the time of love, these three dimensions take center stage in the success or failure in marriage. During the stage of courtship, there is no embarrassment to call off the relationship if any of these three attributes are absent or tenuous. One must be certain that these three qualities are present in good measure. If there is no respect for one another, it is but a convenient arrangement to save on expenses and grocery bills. Respect is the foundation of admiration of what she stands for and for who she is. Without respect, the reception following the wedding ceremony is but a celebration of the victory dance of winning a trophy wife or the success of seduction. If there is no trust, there is no permanence in the marriage. One can never be sure that your partner will keep the promise s/he made, particularly the one that said, "keep thee only unto her." There will be no assurance that certain things will be done. If s/he cannot be counted on to do his part, one might as well live without him, because he will be but a burden for you. Trust is so vital to a relationship, especially in marriage, that one cannot live with the risk of betrayal. Commitment might be the cement that holds things together when the going get tough. Commitment is that promise made to each other that when problems arise, one will not turn his back on the relationship already formed but will remain to work together to find a solution. This resolution might involve giving up something he has invested heavily. That is the cost of commitment.

Marriage is a serious business. You are making promises that binds you for life. I am impressed with the attention to details given by the bride and groom concerning the decoration of the church and the flower arrangement of the head table. I wish that they spend half the time talking about the obligations they are taking on for each other. This points out the importance and need of premarital counseling classes. I am sure that many couples take it very seriously, but too many come to be married under a cloud of illusion. When asked, "Do you know the typical problem solving style your partner uses when problems arise?" Often they answered, "We love each other very much, and we believe that love conquers all." "But love does not put bread on the table, or buy diapers for three young children." "We'll figure out some way when we come to it."

The institution of marriage is one of the most challenging situations there is. To make it more difficult, it takes place often to people with the least life experience, and driven by hormones and physiological changes in the body. Just think of the situation, here are two persons who come into the present moment with at least twenty years of different ways of doing things, everything from financial management to sleeping habits. It requires a great deal of patience to sync together so that the difference does not become a major issue.

Intrinsic to dealing with differences is the issue of control. There are various level of control, but control starts with very innocent beginning. One learns at a very early time, to exercise control of various kind. We learn to use constraint in our bodily functions. We learn to master the situation until it is convenient for us. Gradually we like to do things when, and how according to our convenience. This can easily lead into the way of social interactions with other people. Some goes to excess in wanting to control every situation so that it fits his convenience. In a marriage situation, every difference involves the temptation to maintain control without consideration of the other person's wishes or preference. The advice is that one does not need to win every skirmish, the war is already won because the final common goals have already been decided, whether it be to provide a healthy environment to bring up the children or to pursue financial stability. The operative words is common goals. Too often, common goals are not explicit, sometimes it is as vague as "I just cannot live without him/her."

I like the plague that I leave hanging on my office wall.

> "I don't want you to walk behind me,
> For I am not looking for a robot.
> I don't want you to walk in front of me,
> For I know my way around..
> I want you to walk beside me,
> I want you to be my partner in life."

This reminder has great value to deal with the issue of control. One should feel free to enjoy independence in a relationship, balanced with togetherness. Therefore the operative word is interdependence. It is difficult to achieve but when it is accomplished, there is harmony and security. There are some who are so "needy" that it borders pathology. During courtship, it is often disguised as attentiveness when two persons are involved emotionally. This is one of the things to scrutinize and be certain that it is possible to have separate lives and interests as well as enjoying each other's company. It is the responsibility of each to respect separateness as well as to expect the joy of being together.

~

# Chapter 26

# Science and religion

Before we get into a serious discussion on science and religion, we must clarify terms and eliminate some of the misnomers that are associated with them. Let us deal with some preliminaries. It is easier to talk about them face to face because we are in the interactive mode. We can stop and ask for clarification on any point that causes confusion or disagreement, but through the written words, our communication is static and only one way. We have no ways to check whether we are on the same page or even the same book. When we have no way to check where we differ, we disengage with each other immediately.

We have religion among us ever since there are humans on earth. Anything we do not understand, we made images and bow down before them, mostly to appease them so that they may not hurt us. Many ancient religions belong to this group.

Religion has been identified as ritual, creed and even superstition. It has been maligned with the mistakes of the past, committed by the organized church. Religion has been linked with denominations, or a particular interpretation of how we should approach the deity. So religion has been used loosely and it is heavily laden with emotions and bias, depending on one's past experience.

To many, religion is so mysterious, it has its own vocabulary,which is not common to everyday usage. Such words as cosmology, transcendence, exegesis, teleology and "rapture" are foreign to the common man. People are slow to learn new things, especially if it does not help them make that extra dollar.

There is much negativism against religion that prejudice us from looking at it with a clear mind. Religion has been made to include much of the evils done to mankind. It has been made responsible for much of the darker side of society. History can never forget the atrocities of the Inquisition of the middle ages and the suppression of the findings of Galileo when the church wants to maintain that the earth is flat.

Science on the other hand has not been spotless. It is seen as the terrible monster that will eventually control our lives and lead us to our own demise. Through the imagination of the fiction writers of Hollywood, their products have been taken as real. We have given too much power to what science can do and bastardize what science really is.

There are extremists in every group. Among their convictions, each side believes in the supremacy of their ideas and cannot be tolerant to think clearly except to pursue their own goals in their own respective fields. The common men have been misled by the extremists in each group and are afraid to search for the answer for themselves.

To many, there is no conflict between the two fields of inquiries, if they only stay on their side of the fence. Science is a method of inquiries, their 'bread and butter' was quantifying results. When there are enough observations to show similarities and correlation, after due analysis, a theory is made to explain certain phenomenon. If it can be replicated to show consistencies and reliability, students use it to explain what they can see, until a better theory is formed. Although they have a hunch what they expect the result to be, they are open minded about the conclusion, but the foremost priority is on consistency and reliability. There is nothing sacred about a theory, which is prompted only by observations. Theories can be replaced the moment a better one is found. For example the laws of gravity is still a theory until a better theory be found. Since it has stood the test of time for thousands of years, and no better theory is forthcoming to explain what they see, it slips into the category of being a law.

No area of life is off limit to scientific inquiry. However, there are certain aspect of life that are not legitimate fields for their study. Such entities like beauty, truth and goodness are beyond their capacity to quantify although their impact on life may be seen and measured. The effort of science should be to concentrate on development of good theory.

Religion has been confused with spirituality. Spirituality is in the realm of pure concept like truth, beauty and goodness. It dwells in the unseen world, it cannot be touched, divided or quantified. In fact, it cannot be captured by men. When men attempt to put it into material form like images rituals and gestures, the inadequacies of linguistics and mind power become evident and fail them from telling the complete truth as it should be told. It is like a blind man trying to paint a picture of a sunset. His best effort will fall short of presenting sunset because he has not experienced the sunset. His perception of the sunset is only in his imagination, consequently he cannot communicate about its true splendour and the essence of the sunset accurately. Thus the pure concept is distorted. Or it is like a young man who just finished his dug out canoe in Africa.

He has yet to learn how to deal with the currents as he crosses the river. Yet he has dreams to circumnavigate the world. What he knows is commendable but has very little in common with the complex system of celestial navigation and ocean currents. If he assumes his present knowledge as complete, then his arrogance has overcome his humility.

So far I described what religion is not. Let me say a word about how we come to this place.

Our mind power limits us to perceive certain concepts as long as we are encapsulated in this body. One example is the way we conceive the deity. It reaches back when polytheism was accepted as the norm. Many find it difficult to conceive the possibility of the Trinity (three in one idea). How can three units be combined into one. It runs contrary to the whole principle in Arithmetic. To make it simple for everybody, they focus on the importance of functionality. They divide the Godhead into three separate entities, the father being the creator, Jesus being the savior and the holy spirit, being the eternal abiding presence of God. Without knowing, they unconsciously revert back to polytheism. This illustrates the basic discomfort of moving into a new mode of thinking when dealing with the other realm of reality called spirituality.

Another simple way to incorporate pagan practices into spirituality is to use naturalism. That is to ascribe normal physical phenomenon as the work of god. Many think of thunderstorm and tsunami as god's way to show his wrath and displeasure to men. Weather science can explain the cause and demystify such mysteries. God has nothing to do with it.

Another way to use naturalism is to multiply our own virtues and project it to God and say god must be like that. ..That is called anthropomorphism.. Motherhood is a beautiful thing. Since our mother is our first teacher, and since Jesus is so good, his mother must have been a saint to have produced a son as wonderful as Jesus. They honor her and count her as someone special among all women. They go one step further and honor her with the title of "Mary,the y ended up deifying her. Thoughtful people would find it less objectionable to call "Mary, mother of God incarnate." Although they distinguish a difference between sacrementals and sacraments, laymen do not draw the fine line between the two. Unfortunately, what started out as honoring Mary, developed into a dogma of the church, making her as an intermediary between God and men. And if Mary is so special, her mother Ann must have been wonderful, so they ended up canonize her to be Saint Ann.

One must remember that the Bible is only a translation from Greek and Hebrew. Keep in mind that Hebrew Scripture do not have punctuation marks. Unless you believe that God dictates the words, including the commas and periods,to the scholars, there is still the possibility of human errors being included. It is important to place the pauses when reading the scripture orally.

For example, there is no comma within the phrase "drink ye all of it" in Matthew 26:26. There are two possible places to pause."drink ye all (pause)...of it" and "drink ye (pause)...all of it." The former case can mean that the invitation is opened to everyone present and no one will be turned away. The latter case can be interpreted as emptying the cup, leaving not a drop inside. Depending where the pause is inserted, the meaning of the phrase is changed.

The central message of the Bible is that God loves us. Though science can neither prove nor disprove that statement, it can still make a contribution to its understanding. It can compliment the scripture by telling us how wonderfully the world was created for men to live in. Thus the Bible can raise the question "what" about the world while science can add the details about "how", about the world's beginning.

Here are two seemingly opposing views. The first book of the Bible, Genesis, states the God created the earth in six days. Science presents evidences through carbon dating that the earth existed for millions of years. If we compare the two statements, what are we to do with the whole field of archeology? Should we dismiss the evidences and deny its findings and say it is the work of the devil to deceive us? If only religion can accept the idea that the Bible is not a textbook of science, science and religion can live in harmony with each other.

Albert Einstein described the relation between science and religion succinctly when he said, "Science without religion is lame, and religion without science is blind."

When we use science to study the vastness of the universe and the precise path of the planets, it helps us to know the wonders of His creation. When we study the mysterious ways the human brain communicates with the rest of the body, or how the brain can logically analyze a complex problem and produce a logical solution, we can add our voices to the angels to sing how wonderfully we are made. Science can enrich our lives. Without science, we would still hunt animals with stumps from a tree and wear their skins on our back and sorcery would be the only means to combat diseases.

Religion on the other hand, tells us of our relationship with the deity. It adds dignity to our lives. Without the moral code, which has its bases on religious truths, there would be no society. We would live a life of barbarism without any respect for the sanctity of life. How impoverished we would be if there is no God. We would have no purpose and reason to live. Science enables us to live a full life. But why should we want to live a long life? Such existential question science is ill equipped to investigate and must turn to religion for guidance. There have been many ways to answer, but the most eloquent answer is given in the catechisms. "To love God and to enjoy Him forever."

~

# Chapter 27

# Making Sense of Religion.

Some of my readers may choose to skip this chapter, especially those who have found their faith and are happy with their religion. This chapter is not meant to proselytize for new converts. My audience is focused toward the young people and others who are confused with the diversity of religious beliefs as they find them. I shall restrict myself to deal only with Christianity. I have little knowledge of other religions such as Buddhism, Islam or Mohammedanism.. If you are interested in comparing them, this chapter is not for you.

Most young people have been brought up in Christian homes and have been exposed to Sunday school, baptized as an infant and even confirmed in the church. As they mature and begin to search for the truth for themselves, they are confused with what they find. There are so many varieties of churches, each claiming to have found the truth. They all cannot be right if there is only one truth. What can they do?

This chapter is meant to provide an overview of the landscape. It does not advocate any particular interpretation to be right, nor does not favor any particular approach. Because everyone is so different.

First we must recognize our different backgrounds and the cultures in which we were nurtured. People have different opinions, preferences, affiliations and priorities. We think differently, have our own personality and comfort zone. Some lean more toward ritualist approach, while others favor intellectual understanding. Some express their feelings with open emotions while others are more sedate in their behavior. Many require more outward rituals to show reverence while others are more thoughtful and meditative in their worship. These differences results in diversity.

Here are some other reasons how we come to this confusion.

So far we have been using the wrong method of approach to access spirituality. We have been using anthropomorphic means to search for God. We take the best of human attributes, multiply it a thousand times and ascribe it to God. It does not work that way. God is spirit and we are humans. We speak and think in a different language. Our mind are limited and cannot think comfortably beyond four dimensions, height, width, length and time. What we have in the scripture is a translation from the Greek and Hebrew. In the process of translation, many times, we cannot find an English word to completely convey the meaning of the original Greek or Hebrew. For example, in the Sermon on the Mount, Jesus said, "Be ye perfect even as your father in heaven is perfect." The Greek word teleos is not translated adequately by the English word perfect, (in terms of sinlessness). Unless the word "perfect" is translated accurately, an impossible task is placed on men to be sinless (as God is sinless). The Greek word means more of destiny, or the purpose for which you are created than without flaw. A dog is perfect if she barks at strangers in your yard even in the early hours of the morning, much to the embarrassment of the owner. The dog is bred to bark and to raise an alarm. Men are created to enjoy God and to serve him. His sinfulness is part of his nature. His highest priority (his destiny) is to serve Him, and the removal of his sinfulness is necessary in order to achieve his destiny. When we focus on the means, we are doomed to fail. If we focus on the destiny, we have a mission to fulfil.

Another example is the word virgin in the phrase virgin birth. The Greek word means only young woman without any sexual reference at all. There are numerous other incidences where the English translation does not capture correctly or adequately,the real meaning of the word.

The English language we use in the Bible has changed through the ages. The word 'want' at the first line of 23rd Psalm never mean "a choice." The English word "lack" is more accurate to our ear and is quite different.

As I survey the landscape of Christianity, there are many interpretations of what they consider as truth.. True historical Christianity insists on a minimum of three articles. First, God is spirit. Second, God is love. Third, in order to live in harmony with him, one must live a restored, redemptive relationship with him. These articles have been thoroughly tested, studied, debated and decided by the councils of the early church in the past. They are incorporated into the creed which was recited every Sunday.

The first article says that "God is spirit." As explained in the previous chapter, we have been using the wrong means to seek God. Remember the blind man and his dugout canoe. Unless we learn and follow his instructions, we will not be successful in finding him. "God is spirit, and they that worship him must worship him in spirit and in truth." John 4:24. We do not hunt a tiger using a carrot stick. We use a proper bait. If God is spirit, we must seek him by using spiritual means.

The second article says that God is love. The old Testament portrait him as one who will deliver them into the promise land. He is a law giver. But Jesus comes to tell us that God is love. He so loved us (John 3:16) that he died on the cross in our place. There is no clearer statement than that. He gave us his life that we may live.

The third article says that to live in harmony with Him, we must live a restored, redemptive life.

There is a phrase among those who work with tools and machinery that is parallel to this metaphysical concept. They call it a sweet spot. It is a point of balance in the case of a tool. It is a sound when the machine is humming at an optimum speed, a balance between input and output of the engine. There is a ratio between width and the length of an object that is most pleasing to the eye. It is called the Fibonacci ratio. There is an emotional feeling of well being when one feels everything is running harmoniously between the self and the world and between self and others and most important of all, between self and the divine. It does not come often but once in a while, one feels that s/he is on top of the world or as some would say, "in the groove." Nature has a way to tell us when we are in perfect balance between saltiness and sweet, a state where it is neither too hot or too cold. In spirituality, we called that 'union with God'. According to those who experience such ecstasy, they called it "born again experience." In this state, one feels everything is in balanced, he is free because his past mistakes are wiped away, s/he is restored from his past sin and regrets. One feels the sweetness of abandonment because s/he can casts all his worries on God who will take care of it. His future is assured because s/he is expected at the banquet table which is prepared for him. Such journey is described as living in faith.

This promise is hard earned. Jesus paid for this with his own life on the cross. That is why a crucifix is kept in many churches. It is a powerful image to remind the converts that their freedom is paid for by someone. The crucifix also say to us, "think about the love I have for you. I suffer in your place, I gave my life for you. Look at me, think of the shame I bore for you, I died as as a criminal, so you can go free. Does it mean nothing to you?"

I quote from one of my favorite hymns:

" See from His head, His hands, His feet,
Sorrow and love flow mingled down!
Did e'er such love and sorrow meet,
Or thorns compose so rich a crown?

Divine so amazing, so divine,
Demands my life, my all."

Each one must find his/her comfort zone in their religious practices. The different sweet spot permits us to have diversity. Remember, don't throw the baby out as you empty the dirty water in the pan.

~

# Chapter 28

## Fun time, old hobbies.

Shortly after Chester and his wife arrive to Salisbury North Carolina, he had notions of liquidating his real estate and consolidate his holdings. He wanted to turn the fifteen acres of farmland in New York state into building lots. He anticipated that the whole project could be finished in three years time. It happened during the time of the economic downturn and the process took much longer than the time allotted. His surveyor, who did the work suggested that he take out an bank loan to pay for his service. Whether through a loan or a credit card, Chester still had to think of a way to pay for this sum. He recalled the idea, that this was the Gold Mountain, that if one was willing to work hard, one should be able to achieve his goal. He also recalled somewhere at the back of his mind, the saying that all work was honorable. So he decided that the simplest way to earn extra cash without capital investment was to wash windows for businesses on Main Street. With an investment of twenty eight dollars to buy a bucket and brushes, he started the business with a monthly revenue of two hundred dollars. Thirteen months later, his income grew to one thousand dollars a month. Chester sold the business to a contractor in a nearby town for three thousand dollars. With this money he paid off his surveyor in full and enrolled in the truck driving school in order to get his commercial driving license. In due time, he apprenticed himself to an 18 wheeler driver through a trucking company. He was mentored by a senior driver and they were assigned to a night run between York, Pennsylvania and Columbia, South Carolina for the Caterpillar Tractor Company. His instructor was one of the few non-smoker employees with this trucking company. After the night delivery, they would pick up a load of newsprint around Savannah and delivered it to West Virginia. That was a typical run. During their association together, he learned a great deal from him. They shared many experiences together including some horror stories which happened on the road. He told Chester enough to convince him that truck driving must be one of the most dangerous jobs available. There was an outstanding case that involved one of my own trainee. He was a good driver. One day he was carrying a heavy load on a hilly terrain. As soon as he reached the top of a hill, he saw a disable truck in the middle of the three lane highway. The momentum from the weight of the cargo prevented him from stopping in time. There was traffic on both sides of the highway and it was impossible to take evasive action. So the inevitable accident took place. The company absolved its responsibility by saying to the driver, "You are not in complete control of your vehicle." That situation happen more often than you imagine. You are taking your future in your own hands when you drive among poor drivers on the road."

"That is scary to be in that sort of situation.

"It is one thing to buy insurance to protect yourself, it is another thing to be involved with a fatality of the other driver. You have to live with the thought that someone lost a father, or a husband, or a son."

"That is a sobering thought."

Soon after that conversation , Chester looked elsewhere for a driving position. He interviewed for an independent contractor job transporting school buses to the customer. They paid a flat rate for the job, and the driver was responsible for all expense except the gasoline. He felt that was too independent for an operator and he was not ready to survive on the road on his own. When he returned for the final paper signing, the decision was taken out of his hand. The head office reported that their insurance coverage did not cover a driver of his age. Secretly, he was happy he did not have to decline.

Next he got a job driving cars within the auction house ground, driving vehicles to the auctioneer's line in a building, and to return the vehicle back to the original position on the lot. Unbeknown to him, his cataracts were becoming a problem. He was involved in an accident and was terminated from the company. Meanwhile he had volunteered his service to the nearby airport, filling the "information desk" vacancy. Soon there was an opening in the ranks of the shuttle bus drivers. It was a simple run between the terminal and the parking lots, during the second shift. Chester met some very nice coworkers as well as some steady customers. It was a very pleasant experience, until the price of gasoline rose above three dollars a gallon. By that time, it was prohibitive to drive one hundred twenty miles to earn minimum wage. Reluctantly he resigned his position with the airport and "retired actively."

Chester always believed in learning new skills. It had always been a mystery about electronic programming. How could one manage to arrange "0's and 1's" in such a way to convey a message or to do other things? So he enrolled into the electronic program at the local community college. His first introduction was a course in soldering. Little did he know that there was a correct way to solder properly. It was a fun course and free, since Chester had passed his 65th birthday by then. This opened a whole new field of electronic technology which had always interest him since childhood. The next course after the soldering class was Boolean Algebra which solved the mystery how zero and one can be turned into programming language. Of course, he had to follow up with courses in programming which included C++. It even led him to pursue courses of advance programming in the nearby college sixty miles away.

Chester remembered the first assignment. "Write a program for a four direction traffic light."

After a little thinking, Chester wrote the following "paper." First, there were five scenario to the problem. Secondly, label the four faces as A, B, C and D each facing the four roads of the intersection. Thirdly, light A and light C were controlled by the same switch, while light B and light D were connected to the same switch. Fourthly, there were sensors buried 1,500 ft before the light in the ground. Fifthly, there was a control panel to which all switches and sensors were connected.

The first scenario started with light A and C showing a red light while light B and D showed green. When light A or C sensor detected a vehicle overhead, it activated the switch, the control panel moved to the second scenario.

The second scenario turned on the caution light at light B and D for 10 seconds. The lights A and C still showed red. After the elapsed time, the third scenario was activated.

The third scenario turned light B and D to red while light A and C turned to green.

The fourth scenario was activated when light B or D sensor detected a vehicle passing over it. This triggered light A and C to switch on the caution light for 10 seconds. After the elapsed time had passed, the system proceeded to the fifth and last stage.

The fifth scenario switched light B and D to green and light A and C to red. This would continue until light A or C sensor detected motion overhead. This sequence repeated itself.

This was the first assignment. Other variations followed: Write a program when light A faced a main thoroughfare and light C is secondary road. Increase the caution light by 15 seconds.

The second variation dealt with a situation where the main traffic faced light A, it now had a backup line of two miles. Meanwhile traffic facing light B was building up. Write a program controlling this intersection giving priority to the main traffic facing light A, and interrupt light A traffic every 60 seconds to allow traffic facing light B to go for 15 seconds.

Those were the class exercises for the whole semester. It taught sequential thinking, partializing problems and interrelationships between many components and contingencies planning.

Chester learned enough to work with an electronic technician who had a contract with a weaving company who used electronic circuit board to control their looms. He assisted him to troubleshoot the circuit boards and replace the short circuited components. Some of the malfunctioning parts were caused by workers who still spit from chewing tobacco. It was a humorous way to earn a living, living off the ills of some barbaric practices of the middle ages. This contract came to an end when Cone Mill was forced to consolidate operation and moved the manufacturing plant in a nearby bigger city, Greensboro, NC.

~

# Chapter 29

# Retirement

The traditional bicycle put the rider on top of the two wheels. Chester found it too uncomfortable to ride for any distance. He was leaning toward the handlebar which put weight on his forearms. His shoulders became very sore. Meanwhile he was sitting on a very narrow saddle seat. Some called such seat no better than a 2X4. Because Chester had a extra long tail bone it was unbearable to sit for any length of time. The solution to these problems was to ride in a recumbent bicycle. The two wheels of the cycle were stretched to allow the rider to sit between them.. He was only six to eight inches from the ground. This added to the stability of the vehicle. If he happened to fall, he could easily put his foot on the ground. Falling eight inches to the ground was much better the 36 inches. Instead of pushing his feet downward on the pedal, the rider was pushing his feet forward with his back supported by a back rest. This was very popular in Europe but had not been widespread in America. There were manufacturers on the west coast but the cost was prohibitive for Chester's pocket. The only solution was to make one for himself. Since he had taken courses in welding, he was pleased to think that he had the basic skill to make such a bicycle. Chester obtained plans from the internet and compared them for simplicity and overall appearance. He consulted his old instructor in welding and asked for his advice. Mr. Thompson thought it was do-able. That was a final course available in the program in which a student could do an independent study to demonstrate his overall skill and knowledge. Chester was thought to have a basic skill in welding to profit from such endeavor. He was given permission to register for this course.

At the registration desk, the community college had no record of his attendance over fifteen years ago. So it was necessary to enroll him as a new student. The clerk was building up his profile as a new student. The questionnaire asked for the typical background information. It wanted to document the schools he attended starting with elementary and high school. She asked what year he graduated and wanted to see proof of his graduation from high school. Chester confessed that it was so long ago, that he forgot which year it was, let alone be able show his high school diploma. That created a big hurdle and the computer could not allow the clerk to proceed without proof of his high school graduation. No amount of persuasion satisfied her nor the computer. Even the fact that he had earned three graduate degrees, not even a Ph.D. would do the trick. After much negotiations, he asked to see her supervisor. Although she was willing to make an exception, the registration could not be completed. And the college could not be reimbursed for such a student. The supervisor agreed to contact the instructor to see what could be arranged. The matter was left in mid air until he was told that arrangements has been made.

The local recycling yard put away all the old bicycles for Chester and the list was completed.

The project involved bending the main strut made of two and half inch steel pipe. Fortunately such material was available and the machine bent the pipe like butter. After the rear wheel casing was made, then the braking system was put in place. The seat and the steering column and the front wheel were installed. The total out of pocket expense was twenty six dollars to buy three links of bicycle chains, and extra cable to connect the brakes to the hand bar. The welding was completed and road tested by one of the classmates.

The experience of learning to ride this bicycle began. Involved was the psychological learning to steer the bicycle. Normally the steering process was an unconscious process. The brain sensed the need to change direction to avoid collision with an object or to keep from running into the gutter. When Chester learned to ride this recumbent bicycle, he found himself having to make conscious effort to turn the steering wheel. When he realized that this turning process was no longer done automatically he concluded that his cycling days were over. But it gave him bragging rights and a good story to tell.

Ever since Chester was ten years old, he took whatever material there was on hand and tried to make things with it to amuse himself. He remembered very clearly his attempts to keep the twines from unraveling. The only twines available was from packaging from the meat market. They were soft without any body. He would take thread and whip the end. He spent many hours doing the same thing with twines and thread and never forgot the satisfaction he felt to have that accomplishment. Nearly seventy years later, now that he had the time and the opportunity to have any size of rope and cordage he needed, Chester decided to revive this long held ambition by doing it properly like the sailors of ancient time. He did some research on the internet and read some books from the library and became addicted to this art form. Finally he located someone who sold the cordage that was suitable for tying knots. Chester contacted him by phone and arranged to meet him in person. Martin became a good friend since that first meeting. He was a retired petty officer of the Coast Guard. He was very helpful to get him started and actually demonstrated how the star knot was tied. He also showed him some of the knots he had done, that really set Chester on fire and his interest in knot tying took off.

Knot tying has a long history. At one time it was practiced among sailors during the clipper ship era. They were mostly illiterate but they had much idle time on their hand and there were always ropes around them. They would tie decorative knots and when they arrived at a port, they would sell their craft. They would also seek out other sailors to exchange their latest discoveries and their knowledge of knots. It was becoming a lost art but there were still enthusiasts who practiced this art form.

Fortunately, he found more help through contact with other enthusiasts. It was one thing to read the instruction "to place the working end under this loop", but to be able to see which of the two ends the author was referring to and which of the possible three loops he had in mind. It was too confusing for Chester, being a visual person. Usually the instructions were too terse. There were many cardinal rules in knot tying. For example, "Don't try to tighten the knot all at one time. Generally you will save

time in the long run if you do it in three small increments."
This is the only way to keep symmetry in your knot.
Symmetry is the number one attribute when tying knots.   It
is the result of a very sensitive amount of pull on the cord
when you took out the slack.  You began to develop this
feel after you mastered the mechanics of doing the knot,
(until you can go on autopilot) after the hundredth time.
Unless you have lots of time and patience, don't take up this
hobby.  When it was done properly, the presentation was a
thing of beauty and awe inspiring.

There were a few fundamental knots which were
considered the building blocks from which other more
complicated knots were made.  Simple components of knots
were crown knots, wall knots, Matthew Walker knots and
diamond knots, just to name a few.  Chester favorite knot
was the star knot.  It could be made with any number of
strands.  He had experimented with six, up to ten.  But at
the end, five strands were used, because it was most
manageable, simple and elegant.  It was made with walker
and crown knots and other combinations of weaving the
strands, through and over each other.  He must have been
tying this for the two hundredth star knots by now and he
was still learning subtle ways of improving it.

There were always new terminologies to learn in any
art form.  In knot tying, such words as loops, end, bights
and others needed to be mastered.  It was an art to be able to
transfer in your mind an image from a two dimensional
description into a three dimension object.

There were many other interests in Chester's life.  For
a long time, he had been fascinated with wood turning with
a lathe.  One year, he attended a woodworking trade show
in which equipments were featured.  Included was a booth

sponsored by local woodworking club. There were demonstrations of what could be done with a piece of wood on a lathe. An outstanding exhibit was a cowboy hat being turned from one solid block of wood. That caught his interest and peeked his curiosity to no end. The conversation with the wood worker resulted in an ongoing friendship. He invited Chester to visit his workshop. It was most impressive to see every kind of equipment one would ever dream of. He generously invited him to try his hand in turning simple objects. From there he graduated to try more complicated projects. True to Chester's character, he asked himself what would happen if he tried to do this instead of that? This led him to explore for himself such project as multi-axis off-centered articles as candlesticks and all sort of weird looking monstrosities. By looking at the internet to see what other wood turners were doing, he came upon the idea of using drill press and fostner bit to made free flowing cube within a cube.

During summer, while he was looking for some raw material to make a cane for his brother-in-law, he became friends with a wood worker who experimented with Chester how to bend laminated pieces of wood around a jig to form the handle of the cane. This friend was a retired electrical contractor who equipped himself with a complete woodworking shop. He once submitted six pieces of his collection to the state fair. And he took five first prizes and one second prize that year. For the first time in his life, Chester saw a vase made after the fashion of open segment pattern. It was most exquisite with a light shining from the bottom in a darken room. He taught Chester the secret and the fine points of making jigs to replicate segments for such a project. From then on, Chester continued the search for himself on the internet, how other wood workers had pushed the boundaries in this art form. There was no end to the number of variations one could extend with this idea. To Chester, it was a delight to use wood to reproduce a thirty inch model of a spiral glass light bulb using a compound miter cut. To top it off, Malcolm Tibbitts managed to thread a string of LED light through the middle to make it glow like a light bulb.

There is no end to what could be made with wood and proper tools in the hands of skilled craftsmen with imagination and a touch of curiosity. Life is full of opportunities to discover new things and to live a life with no dull moments.

~

# Chapter 30

# My heroes

I have my kind of hero.  Among them, two names stand out.  One is the dog trainer, Cesar Milan, originally from Mexico.  He started out being an illegal immigrant, and was abandoned by his guide to whom he paid for a contract.  He crawled through tunnels, slept under highway abutments. and many other hair raising experiences which we will never get to hear about.  But his dream still burned in his heart.  He started out to earn his living by just walking dogs for urban dwellers.  Now anyone can do that, if you are willing to work below minimum wage.  He didn't stay there, his dream became his passion.  He worked hard and he prevailed.  We don't know what else he did to survive. But he never lost sight of his goal.  He sought to be the best he could be in his field.  He was gradually recognized and became a top TV personality, successful in his field, seen by viewers all over the world..  He is a good dude with a net worth of over 45 million in his account as last reported.

What you may not realize is that there are many in this world who love to help people who have guts and determination.  We love an underdog, a fighter, someone who knows what he wants and is willing to go after it.  We want to be certain that he is not a shister, looking for a handout.  But if you are able to show what you have done toward your goal, and have a plan, there are enough people to give you a helping hand.  I speak from experience.

Another personality is General Colin Powell. Born in New York city, a self admitted average C student in school but distinguished himself to became a four star General. I am sure he had to overcome many social obstacles before he went to the top in his field. I tip my hat to you, Sir.

My second point is this, particularly to the younger generation and to those who feel that they have been "dealt a wrong hand" in life. The United States is a land of opportunities. That is why it is known to some as "the Gold Mountain." There are many who make their living trying to provide you with the motivation to improve yourself. The bottom line of their message is that you have the power within you to do whatever you decide. You are the captain of your ship and you can determine your own destiny. Don't forget that you are surrounded by "a great cloud of witnesses" who are supporting you spiritually. They are your grandmothers, your aunts and uncles, your parents who are patiently waiting for you to wake up the dragon within you. There is much rejoicing when you succeed, even in small steps, toward your destiny. There is more help available than you realize, when you are serious about your future. You have to do your part and let others know that you mean business.

Take heart my fellow Americans. the United States of America is the best place where you can live out your dreams. If you can dream it, you can do it.

~

# Chapter 31

## Anecdotes

There are things in one's life that are treasured in the inmost sanctum of one's heart.  These are incidents or nicnacs that are meaningful and are kept under lock and key until very special moments.  One shares them only on special occasions.  They include such things as the first sound of the first born at birth for the mother or the wedding dress of a grandmother.

To me, there are three such memories.  First was the way my grandfather sharpened my pencil.  With deftness, he took the knife out of his pocket and began to shape the pencil, exposing just enough lead; shaved the wood around it with  perfect symmetry as if it was cut by a pencil sharpener.  He had a lot of practice for he was the bursar of a high school in Kowloon, the peninsula attached to the Hongkong colony.

The second special memories was the first time my grandmother explained to me the meaning of the family name "Louie."  Through a story, she told me, "it was my ancestor greeting me when I hear the ring of the thunder."  What a wonderful way to teach me to remember my roots.

The third incident was related to writing. When I attended the preparatory school attached to the high school at which my grandfather was the bursar, there were composition classes in which students turned in a weekly exercise. After using the narrative form for a long time, I decided "just for a lark," why don't I introduce some dialogue with the gardener in the composition. Up to that time, I have been receiving a B grade. For the first time, I was rewarded with an A. I said to myself, "if that's what it takes to get an A, I can put a lot of dialogue into every exercise."

That was the beginning of my exploiting dialogue in my writing. Through it, I can introduce a wider horizon to the subject matter and explore in depth the subject at hand. I can do all that by making the other person asks the question. What a powerful tool I can use! It is a natural way to develop the idea of "presence" in my writing. Instead of just talking at the reader, I can bring him with me into the situation.

Another outstanding incident happened when I was in Toronto being trained as a Met. Officer. I attended a "large city church" on Bloor Street. E. Crossley Hunter was the preacher. Through conversation with him, he shared with me his success and approach to preaching. He said, "Relate profundity with simplicity. Speak on profound topics in simple way that common men and women in the pews can understand. I am not afraid to grapple lofty themes and profound mysteries of the divine. But I always keep the common men in my focus. Include such weighty phenomena as cosmology and sanctification in the homily, but put them in such a way that a grade six student can follow. That's what good preaching is all about."

I never forgot that conversation and tried always to practice that faithfully for the last twenty-six years in my ministry.

~

# Chapter 32

## Finally

A dragon is a mythical creature, and one can never tame a wild beast. The best one can do is to learn how to ride it and use it to help one achieve his goal before he gets thrown off the back. One can never divest completely your heritage, your mother tongue and your values. They are the fibers of your being. Incidentally, often I still find myself reverting to Chinese when I use the multiplication table. You can imagine how many times a day that happens.

I am extremely grateful beyond words for what I received, surrounded with good and generous friends and mentors, and above all, endowed with a good dose of curiosity. The pursuit to know the hows and the whys of things keeps my mind active and alert. I am not the fastest learner on earth, but I learned to compensate with persistence and commitment to the goal, like taking seven road tests before I got my motorcycle license. For an immigrant, I didn't turn out too shoddy.

None of these would have happened without a good woman in my life. She is extremely talented, plays several musical instruments, and is a respected professional in her own field of nursing. Above all, she is highly intelligent. Therefore, my very last word of this book (I promise) would be to give much of the credit to my partner and my wife, Allene. Truly, she is "the wind under my wings."

~